YOU CAN COOK ANYTHING CHINESE!

Madame Yee Yo

HILIT PUBLISHING COMPANY, LTD.
TAIPEI
HIGHLIGHT INTERNATIONAL, INC.
ARLINGTON, VA

THE CHINESE TRANSLATION:

簡易中國菜

ALSO IN THE FOURTH EDITION

FRENCH EDITION, 1988

Revised Edition: January, 1994
HILIT PUBLISHING COMPANY, LTD.
3rd Fl. No. 1 Sec. 4, Hsin-Yi Road, Taipei 10656, Taiwan, R.O.C.

Publisher's Cataloging-in-Publication Data:
Yee, Yo.
    You can cook anything Chinese!/ Yee Yo. – –
Rev. ed. – – Taipei, Taiwan: Hilt Pub. Co.;
Arlington, VA: Highlight International, Inc., [1992]

    p.   ;   ill.;   cm.
    "April; 1992" – – T.p. verso.
    Includes index.
    ISBN: 0-914929-91-7

    1. Cookery, Chinese.   I. Title.
TX724.5.C5Y44   1992   641.592'951 dc20
                          93-80A62

Publisher   : Dixson D.S. Sung
Author   : MADAME YEE YO
Photographer   : Yu-Ping Lin
Design & Editing   : Highlight International Co., Ltd.
Photography & Printing   : Highlight International Co., Ltd.
Production   : Hilit Publishing Co., Ltd.
Editor   : Brian P. Klingborg
Lithographed in Taiwan, R.O.C.

Dedicated affectionately to
My Loving Husband
GEORGE K. CHACKO
Without whose persuasive push
And strong sustaining support
These culinary delights would have
Continued to remain family secrets

CONTENTS

ACKNOWLEDGEMENTS

It is my pleasure to acknowledge most gratefully the excellent instruction received from my teachers at Hai-Wai Chef's College; the urging of many of my students over the years to write this book; the constant encouragement of Lang Lee and Lillian Namrow; the careful reading of the manuscript by Linda and David Ludwig, Gail and Constance Woods and Anne Edwards; the verification of historical references by Chang Shu-lin, Tsuang Hung-yi, and Lai Yue Jen; the counsel of Chu Ho on cooking methods; and of son Rajah Y. Chacko on linguistics; the careful proofreading by daughter Ashia Chacko and nephew Anthony Swei; the professional photography and production by Hilit Publishing Company; and above all, the untiring accomplishment of tasks, lowly and lofty, from start to finish, by husband George K. Chacko, to whom I joyfully dedicate this book.

PREFACE

Time and again, I have been encouraged by my students at the Yee Yo Chinese Cooking School to write a cookbook. They say to me, "Your recipes are marvelous, and foolproof, too!"

My students learn traditional Chinese cooking in a non-traditional way. Instead of learning to cook food by groups, such as soups, vegetables, or meat, they learn Cooking by Methods.

There are several advantages to Cooking by Methods. Once you learn the method of stir-frying, you can stir-fry chicken, beef, pork, and fish in essentially the same way. Also, you can plan menus to emphasize contrasts in taste, color and texture. A steamed dish, no matter what meat or vegetable you use, is usually mild in taste, soft in texture, light in color, and chunky. A stir-fried dish is usually the opposite. Thus, a steamed dish and a stir-fried dish provide you with rich contrasts in taste, texture, and so on. With Cooking by Methods, you can also use your time more wisely. For example, steamed dishes can be prepared in advance and left in the steamer, leaving you free to do some last minute stir-frying. Another advantage is that you learn to use your utensils efficiently — instead of using just one method which forces you to prepare one dish at a time, you can use several methods and create an entire meal all at once.

There are over 60 Chinese cooking methods. Unfortunately, they often overlap. The rather loose way the various methods are organized confuses even native Chinese.

By rather carefully studying the varied cooking terms, and identifying the methods which are most often used, I have been able to come up with 11 Primary Methods and 8 Auxiliary Methods.

The hundreds of questions that my students have raised seem to be best grouped under: *The How and Why of Chinese Cooking.* Among the questions you will find answered are:

* How to make vegetables crisp.
* How to "give my love a chicken that has no bones."
* How to cook Chinese food on an electric stove.
* How to freeze *Wontons.*
* How to make meat tender and velvety.
* How to cook Chinese food when you don't have much free time.
* How to cook just for one person.
* How to bone a chicken breast in less than one minute.
* How to steam without a steamer.

* How to deep-fry.
* Why is home-cooking different from restaurant-cooking?
* Why is tea always served in Chinese restaurants?
* Why can't you double a stir-fried recipe?
* Why are there so many dishes at one meal?
* Why do you chop and chop to cook Chinese food?
* Why is there no centerpiece at a Chinese dinner table?
* Why is the cleaver so clever?

A total of 11 *categories of methods* are discussed. Stir-frying is more than a method, it is a category of methods. There are several variations to the basic method of stir-frying with oil in the wok, including differences in the timing and differences in the sauces. When a dish is prepared using more than one category of methods, it is classified under the primary category. Thus, chicken which is first cured, then steamed, and then smoked, is classified under the Category of Smoking, because it is the smoking which gives it its unique character.

One of the things that my students have found particularly useful is my *grouping of ingredients.* For example, in my recipe for Lemon Chicken, the ingredients for the Lemon Sauce are arranged in order of their use. I start with broth mixed with cornstarch, because cornstarch mixes best with clear liquid. I add dry ingredients first; next, wet ingredients. In this way measuring spoons do not have to be cleaned and dried twice. Similarly, the ingredients of the marinade are arranged in order of their use. Since the two groupings are shown separately, there is no fear of mix-ups or misses.

You want to enjoy your dinner — not just cook it. That means you should have time to enjoy it. A number of choices under different categories of methods are offered, so that you can select a judicious mixture to achieve the Chinese ideals of cooking *Se* (Color); *Hsiang* (Fragrance); and *Wei* (Taste). Sprinkle your delicious offerings with appropriate dashes of knowledgeable comments on particular dishes, ranging from Ma Po Bean Curd to Laba Porridge.

IN THE KITCHEN

CLEAVER CUTTING METHOD

Don't be afraid to use the cleaver. My daughter Ashia was using it at age seven. When you use it correctly, it shouldn't cut you. But don't bet on it! Here is how to use the cleaver correctly:

① Press the item to be cut against the cutting board with the left hand (my apologies to lefties). ② Curve the left fingers so that the tips of the finger nails rest on the item. ③ Cut with the right hand by holding the corner of the blade with the thumb and the index finger and holding the handle with the other three fingers. ④ The right hand cuts while the left hand moves backward. The side of the blade slides up and down against the first and the second knuckles but never rises above the second knuckle so you don't cut yourself.

Semi-frozen or semi-thawed meat is much easier to cut. Freeze meat in sticks approximately 1″ × 2″ for easy cutting.

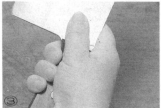

SLICING

Vertical Slicing: Perpendicular to the board, the blade moves in an up-and-down motion. Most meat is cut this way. The usual size of meat slices is approximately 2″ × 1″ × 1/8″. ⑤ Beef must be sliced against the grain, otherwise it will be tough. Slice fish with the grain into thick slices about 1/4″ or thicker so that it will not fall apart when cooked. You don't need to pay much attention to the grain of pork and chicken.

Diagonal Slicing: The blade moves in the same manner as in Vertical Slicing except that the blade meets the item at a 30° angle. ⑥ Stick-shaped vegetables such as carrots, asparagus, etc. are cut this way into 1/8″ slices, thus making oval slices out of round sticks.

Horizontal Slicing: Lay the item flat and hold the cleaver on a slant or parallel to the item. ⑦ Raise the thumb and the pinky and slice carefully so that you won't cut your left hand. This method is used to make wider slices out of flat pieces such as a thin chicken breast or vegetables like celery and bell peppers.

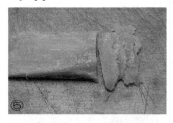

SHREDDING

⑧ When you pile a few slices up and slice them again you make shreds.

When you shred ginger, cut the shreds as fine as you can so that it will not taste too hot when you bite it.

Before you shred scallions, ⑨ smash them with the flat side of cleaver. ⑩ Slice horizontally. ⑪ Cut diagonally into very fine shreds.

DICING

⑫ Dices are made by cutting across thick shreds. Diced pieces should measure 1/2″.

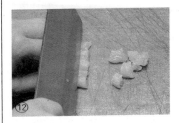

CUBING

⑬Cubes are like dices, except larger. Cubes are used for stewed or sweet and sour dishes.

ROLL-CUTTING

Stick-shaped vegetables such as carrots and gherkins are often roll-cut, not to puzzle the guests, but to create effects that ordinary cubes or slices do not. Roll-cutting exposes more surface area to absorb seasoning. Another advantage to roll-cutting is that the size can be kept uniform. Suppose you slice a carrot, the slice cut from the larger end can be many times as large as the one from the smaller end, although the thickness is the same. This is not so when you roll-cut. Here is how to do it: Place the vegetable on the far side of the cutting board, ⑭ make a diagonal cut, ⑮ roll the vegetable a quarter turn toward you, ⑯ make another diagonal cut, continue the same process until you come to the end. The finished product should line up like "little maidens all in a row."

USING THE FOOD PROCESSOR

A food processor can be very useful in Chinese cooking. It not only saves cutting time, but also makes food taste better whenever ground meat is called for. Meat ground by a grinder does not have the same pleasant texture as meat chopped by hand or by food processor. The following is what a food processor can do as successfully as a cleaver:

MINCING: Chop food into chunks by hand, then mince with steel blade with on/off turns. Avoid over-processing. See p. 14 for processing meat.

SLICING: Many Chinese vegetables are cut into oval-shaped slices. If you don't mind round slices, use a medium or fine slicing disc for slicing vegetables.

Cut meat along the grain into sticks smaller than the feed tube so that when you slice, it will be cut across the grain. Partially freeze or thaw for slicing. Use medium slicing disc.

SHREDDING: For most Chinese dishes, vegetables shredded by shredding and julienne disks are too thin. Instead, use a medium slicing disk and slice food first. Then, stack up the slices and slice again to make shreds. Meat must be partially frozen or thawed. Stack up sliced meat quickly and slice again before it is completely thawed.

BONING

HOW TO BONE A CHICKEN BREAST

① Tear off the skin either before or after boning if skinned meat is called for. ② Tear the meat from the joint bone with fingers. ③ With one hand holding the bone, and the other hand on the meat, pull them apart. ④ Free the meaty part with fingers while pulling so that the meat will come off in one piece. ⑤ Take off white tendon attached to meat by holding the tendon with one hand and scraping the meat off with the other with a knife. Arrange meat between wax paper, wrap in individual packages for each recipe and freeze.

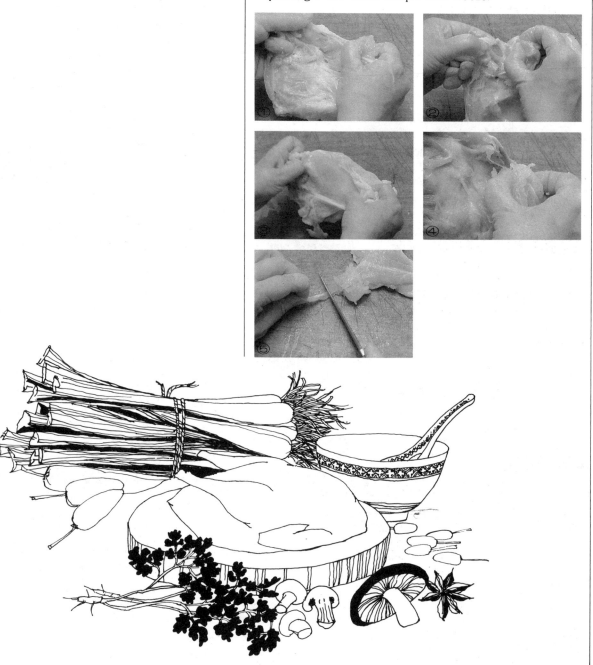

HOW TO BONE A WHOLE BIRD

"I gave my love a chicken that had no bones."

It is always festive to serve a stuffed, boned duck or chicken. It takes a beginner 20 minutes to bone a bird, but only 10 minutes or so for an experienced person.

The task is to separate the meat and the skin from the carcass. Try to keep the skin intact, but if it is accidentally broken, sew it together with a needle and thread. Here is how you bone:

Rinse the fowl, remove loose fat. ① Cut the neck skin off, leaving 1 inch for sewing. ② Peel the skin on one side to expose the wing joint. ③ Wiggle the wing to locate the joints. ④ Cut through the joint to detach the wing from the carcass but leave the wing intact. Repeat with the other wing. ⑤ Pull and tear the skin and meat downward from the carcass, as if you were peeling the skin off a banana. ⑥ Use a small knife to make small snips to free the meat only when necessary, particularly when you are working on the back. ⑦ Free meat around the thigh and drumstick. ⑧ Using a kitchen shear or cleaver, cut through the leg bone. The thigh and leg meat stay with the meat and skin and the thigh bone and the upper part of the leg bone stay with carcass. Continue to peel until you come to the tail-bone. ⑨ Carefully cut the tail bone so that the tail stays with the meat and skin. Now you have completely separated the meat and skin from the carcass. ⑩ Turn the right side of the skin out. Now you have a rather sad looking bird, but it will look all right after it is stuffed. With needle and thread, repair any part of skin that may have been cut accidentally. Lay bird on breast and stuff the upper opening. ⑪ Close opening by sewing. ⑫ Turn bird and repeat with the lower opening.

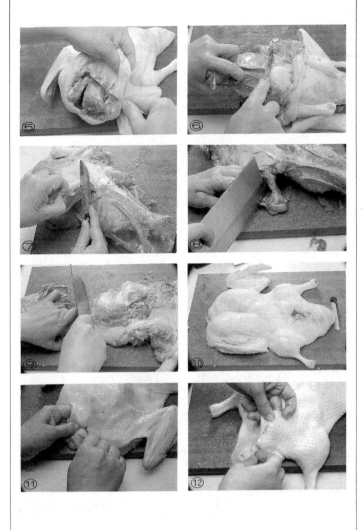

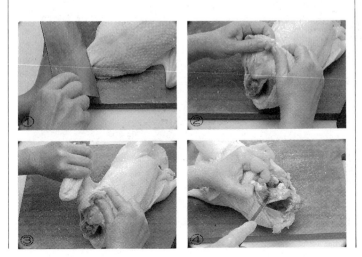

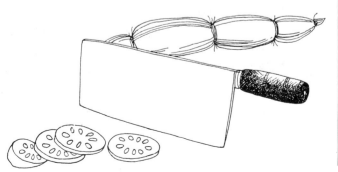

HOW TO CHOP AND ARRANGE A COOKED BIRD

① Separate wings from body. ② Separate thighs from body. ③ Split breast. ④ Open bird and cut through back. ⑤ Work on one half at a time: separate breast portion from the back. ⑥ Chop across breast, either with the bones or without, into 3/4″ strips. ⑦ Arrange in a bowl with skin side down. Separate legs from thighs. Chop thighs into strips and arrange alongside the breast pieces. Chop legs and wings. Use them to fill the bowl. ⑧ Cover bowl with serving platter. ⑨ Invert. ⑩ Remove bowl.

Half of a bird can be cut and arranged in the same way.

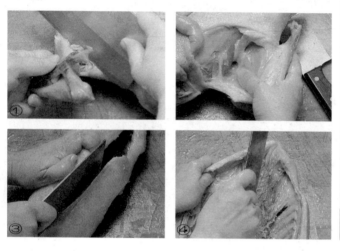

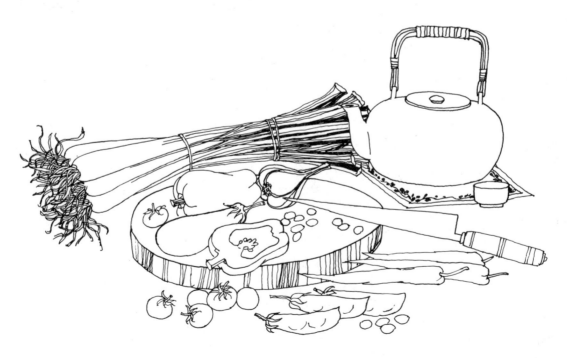

CLEAVER WORK FOR THE CLEVER
THE ALL-PURPOSE CLEAVER

An all-purpose cleaver is indeed all-purpose. In addition to its many uses in cutting, the cleaver can be used also for:

TENDERIZING

① Use the blunt edge to pound meat in criss-cross lines. ② Or use the side to smash meat, garlic, ginger, scallion, etc.

CRUSHING

③ Put a clove of unpeeled garlic on a cutting board and smash with flat side of the cleaver. ④ The skin will come loose easily. ⑤ Crush Sichuan peppercorns or fermented black beans by placing them in a bowl and turning the cleaver vertically, using the handle as a pestle to crush the item.

CHOPPING BONES

Chop chicken, duck and fish bones with the cleaver. ⑥ Just aim at where you wish to chop and give it a decisive bang. You may wish to hide your other hand at this moment! Avoid hitting any spot more than once as this will shatter the bone and make many splinters. ⑦ If you are chicken yourself, position the cleaver on the bird first and hit it with a hammer or the back of another cleaver. Don't use an all-purpose cleaver to cut pork or beef bones. The hard bones can easily damage the blade.

MINCING

Cut food into small pieces, then chop it with an up-and-down motion. ⑧ If you have two cleavers, mince with both of them, like a drummer beating the drums with both hands. Enjoy the beautiful rhythm!

To prevent crunchy items such as water chestnuts and bamboo shoots from flying all over, ⑨ smash them with side of cleaver before mincing.

TRANSFERRING

⑩ After cutting, use the cleaver to scoop the food with one hand, while using the other hand to help. Food can be easily transferred to bowls or utensils this way.

NOT A WEAPON

However all-purpose a cleaver may be, it is not a weapon. You may not hit your spouse if you get angry with him or her. Remember that the Chinese are a non-violent people and it is safe to work in a Chinese kitchen.

HELPFUL HINTS

Here are some tips from years of experience with cooking Chinese food:

BEEF: For Stir-Frying and Plunging, flank or sirloin are the easiest cuts to use. But if you are skillful, cheaper cuts like chuck or round steak can also be used. For Stewing, use chuck or shank.

CHICKEN: Chicken loses its flavor quickly in the refrigerator. Buy it the day you plan to use it. Don't keep it in the refrigerator more than a day. If you must buy it ahead of time, freeze it, provided that it has not been previously frozen.

Buy chicken when it is on sale at a chain store. The chicken will be fresh because the merchandise moves fast when it is on sale. However, beware of "Manager's Specials" which may be a way of getting rid of over-stocked items.

Buy several packages of chicken breasts on sale. Skin and bone the breasts; freeze the meat between wax paper. Make broth out of bones. You can boil down the broth and freeze it also.

Select chicken that is odor-free and clean-looking.

CLAMS: Use only live clams. They are either closed or will close when tapped. Clams that stay open when touched are dead. Live clams open fully when cooked; therefore, discard any closed ones in the pot.

CORNSTARCH: To make sauces, it is easier to mix cornstarch with water or broth before adding it to the other ingredients.

When thickening a sauce with cornstarch paste, always stir the paste before you add it to the sauce.

When marinating, add cornstarch directly to the food to be marinated, either before or after the other ingredients are added.

DIM SUM FREEZING: Freeze *Dim Sum*, such as *Wonton, Jiaotze, Shaomai,* etc. between waxed paper in freezer boxes. Sprinkle paper with flour if frozen raw. Cook or reheat while still frozen, adding 1 to 2 minutes to cooking time. Fried *Dim Sum*, such as Spring Rolls and Shrimp Balls, can be re-heated in a 350°F oven still frozen. But re-frying after thawing is better.

ELECTRIC STOVE: When you need to alternate between high and low heat, keep one burner red-hot and the other medium. Alternate between the two.

For Stir-Frying, heat the burner red-hot before setting the wok on it.

Don't use a collar which will take the wok away from the heat. Instead, use a flat-bottomed wok for Stir-Frying.

FIRE: When the wok or frying pan catches fire, stay calm. It happens often. Simply turn off heat and cover to smother the fire.

FISH: There is no rigid rule as to what kind of fish to use for what kind of method of cooking. In general, fish with tender meat is used for Steaming and Stewing, firm meat for Stir-Frying, Deep-Frying and Curing. Ask the fish salesperson about the texture of the fish. Avoid fish that tends to fall apart when being fried.

Your choice also depends on the size of the fish that will fit your cooking utensil and serving platter. Keep in mind that like seasonal fruit and vegetables, the fish of the season is also the best.

The best fish is fresh fish, which has bulging eyes, bright gills, shiny scales, firm meat, and a fresh smell. Buy fillets that smell fresh. If you are not sure that the so-called "fresh" fillet is really fresh, you'll do better with frozen fillet in packages. Marinate before completely thawed. Keep in refrigerator until ready to use.

When Steaming a fish, you can almost cut the cooking time in half by raising the fish up in the plate with either chopsticks or whole scallions. This allows air to circulate under the fish.

FOOD PROCESSOR: Many recipes which call for ground meat or shrimp can be prepared in the food processor. Set steel blade in place and process whatever ingredients are called for in the following order:

Add slices of ginger first. Mince finely.

Add dried mushrooms (soaked and de-stemmed) and scallions (cut into sections) and mince briefly.

Add meat (cubed) or shrimp, and water chestnuts.

Chop with a few more quick on/off turns.

Do not overprocess the last ingredients.

Add the rest of the ingredients in the group and give another quick on/off turn.

For slicing meat and vegetables, see p.9.

GARLIC: Smash unpeeled cloves of garlic with side of cleaver. This will crush them and loosen their skin at the same time.

GARNISHING: Whenever you prepare food ahead of time and reheat, add green garnish after reheating. Newly garnished dishes have a freshly-made look about them.

GINGER: Don't peel ginger if it is going to be chopped or discarded later. The skin is flavorful. Peel only if ginger shreds are called for.

Use a garlic press to squeeze out the juice when it is called for. Finely chopped ginger can be used in place of juice.

GREEN VEGETABLES: Don't cover green vegetables when cooking, unless they take a long time to cook (i.e. string beans).

GROUND MEAT: Recipes often call for 1/4 pound ground pork or beef. Buy meat in larger quantities, chop and divide into 1/4 pound (1/2 cup) portions. Press down into patties, wrap in plastic wrap and freeze.

INSECTS: In warm climates, insects tend to grow on seeds, grains and certain dried vegetables. Freeze ingredients such as lotus seeds and dried tiger lilies for 48 hours in the spring to discourage eggs from hatching.

LEFTOVERS: Leftover chicken meat can be used in Cold-Mixed recipes (Silver Chicken Threads). Chicken and other kinds of leftovers can be put in Egg Fried Rice or Sour Hot Soup.

MARINATING: There is no need to mix the marinade first and then to add it to the ingredients to be marinated. Just assemble everything in a single operation and mix.

MEAT: Freeze meat for cutting: cut meat along the grain into sticks, approximately 2″ x 1″, and freeze. When you need meat for recipes, partially thaw. You can easily slice against the grain into 2″ x 1″ x 1/8″ slices.

Put small amounts of sliced or shredded meat, marinated or unmarinated, in empty orange juice cans and freeze. Thaw a can whenever you need a small amount of meat for a dish.

OIL: For Stir-Frying and Deep-Frying, use any vegetable oil except olive, coconut or sesame oil. Sesame oil is used mostly for garnish.

Deep-Frying oil can be reused until it is too cloudy. After each frying, let the oil cool. Line a small strainer with a coffee filter. Pour cooled oil into a jar through a strainer. It takes a long time to strain, but the oil will come out clear.

PORK: Fresh pork should look bright and pink. Center-cut pork chops are too lean for most Chinese dishes. Tenderloin is easy to cut for Stir-Frying, but if you have the time and patience to trim the fat off the butt, it will make more tender stir-fried dishes. Use butt also for Barbecued Pork and Sweet and Sour Pork. Use picnic ham or ground pork for Stewing.

For Stir-Frying, marinated pork is more tender, but unmarinated is more flavorful.

RE-HEATING: Re-heat the same way the food was cooked the first time. For instance, re-heat Silver Thread Rolls by Steaming. However, microwave ovens are excellent for re-heating Stir-Fried, Steamed, and Stewed food. Conventional ovens at 350°F are good for re-heating fried food, but it is better to refry.

SCALLIONS: Choose scallions with fresh, green tops and long stems.

Adding scallion at the initial stage of Stir-Frying makes the dish fragrant. Used as a garnish, it adds beauty and a unique fragrance.

Smashing scallions with side of the cleaver makes shredding easier. Smashed scallions release flavor better, too.

No need to cut the scallions into sections for Stewing. You can remove whole scallions easily later.

SEASONING: Salt is the most critical seasoning. Add ½ teaspoon salt or 2 tablespoons soy sauce to each pound of meat or 2 cups broth.

SHRIMP: Only frozen shrimp is available in most supermarkets in the States. Don't mistake the previously-frozen for fresh shrimp. Ask the fish salesperson when the shrimp was thawed. Reject shrimp that has been thawed more than one day. Buy shrimp the day you plan to use it.

The best way to assure that the shrimp is tasty is to buy solid-frozen shrimp and thaw it yourself. Buy a 2-pound or 5-pound box of solid frozen shrimp. Partially thaw in the refrigerator. Hit the box with a hammer to break it loose. Package in 1 pound or 3/4 pound portions in plastic and refreeze. Shell, devein, rinse, and marinate before completely thawed. Buy shrimp frozen in shells. Shrimp frozen without shells rarely has much flavor.

SKIMMING FAT OFF SOUPS AND STEWS: Strain the solids from stock, and refrigerate both separately. Remove fat from stock; then heat stock and solids together.

SOUPS: A few drops of vinegar will enhance the flavor of soups. But don't add too much to make the soup vinegary; exception: Sour and Hot Soup is always vinegary.

THAWING FOOD: Thawed food deteriorates quickly, particularly seafood. Therefore, don't thaw until ready to use. Cut and marinate before completely thawed. Thawing slowly in refrigerator or quickly in microwave oven is better than thawing at room temperature. Avoid thawing in warm water.

WATER CHESTNUTS: Avoid chopping water chestnuts too fine. Coarsely chopped ones are crunchier.

When chopping water chestnuts with cleaver, smash them with the side of cleaver first to prevent the water chestnuts from flying all over.

WOK: Over-scrubbing takes away the much-desired seasoning. Just scrub wok with a plastic, not metal, pad to get rid of food stuck to the wok. You will eventually have a black, non-stick wok.

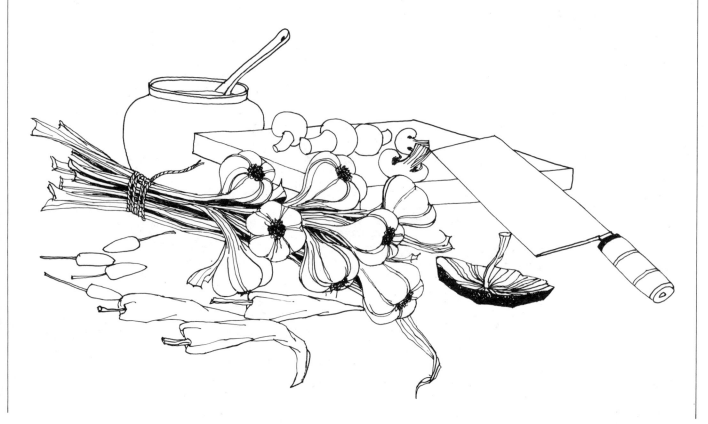

PRIMARY METHODS
STIR-FRYING METHOD 炒

Have you ever taken a peek into the kitchen of a Chinese restaurant? You see the chef juggling many things and tossing everything up in the air. Somehow, everything always lands in the wok! The end result is always perfect — well, almost always.

What you may have witnessed, *Stir-Frying*,** is a method of cooking that is uniquely Chinese. It involves quick tossing of cut-up ingredients into a small amount of oil over intensely hot heat. The majority of Chinese dishes are cooked in this way.

Crackling, 爆 , is Stir-Frying done at lightning speed, usually with bean sauce or a lot of scallions. (See Chicken in Crackling Sauce.)

Dry-Stirring, 煸 , is partially dehydrating the food by slow-stirring in hot oil. (See Fish-Fragrant Eggplant.)

*WHY is Stir-Fried food so attractive, with the meat so tender, and the vegetables so crispy?

A *small* amount of food, tossed *quickly* over *intensely* hot heat makes the meat tender and the vegetables crispy. The cooking is done too quickly to toughen the meat or to make the vegetables wither. The marinating "seals" the juices inside the meat and creates a smooth and velvety texture.

In order to cook quickly and uniformly, the meat and vegetables must be cut into small and uniform pieces. Gas provides the hottest and the most instantaneous heat, making it the best fuel for Chinese cooking. If you have an electric stove, wait until the burner is red hot before putting the wok on. Remove it from the burner when the cooking is done.

Because quick cooking gives the food zest, doubling the recipe will slow down the process and give the food a boiled taste. The overcrowded wok will make the vegetables wither and the meat tough. Therefore, *never double any recipe.* Cook the same recipe twice or more for large groups, but don't double the recipe. Anyway, isn't it better to cook another dish, instead of more of the same? That is one reason why there are so many dishes at a Chinese meal. Besides, the Chinese simply love variety. Furthermore, the more dishes, the higher the honor accorded the guest by the host.

*WHY does my cooking taste different from restaurant food?

Home-style Stir-Frying is different from restaurant-style cooking. At home, the food is tossed in small amounts of oil, while in the restaurant, the vegetables are often first blanched in boiling water, and meats in hot oil, and then both are fried. Restaurants tend to use m.s.g. more often. Also, they add a small amount of previously used oil to the food after it is cooked, so that it will glisten.

You will see that the Gung Bao Chicken recipe is cooked in a modified restaurant-style.

*WHAT is the best oil for Stir-Frying?

Traditionally lard, or a mixture of lard and vegetable oil, was used. Nowadays, vegetable oils are used both at home and in restaurants. All vegetable oils are suitable, except olive oil and Oriental sesame oil. Butter and margarine are not used.

You don't have to juggle a dash of this and a splash of that the way a Chinese chef does in his kitchen. I have measured the ingredients and worked out the timing for you, so that things will turn out just right. In addition, I have grouped the ingredients for your convenience *in order of their use,* like the cast of characters in order of their appearance in a play. They are grouped into dry and wet ingredients, so that you don't have to switch back and forth between cleaning and drying the measuring spoons.

**The name of the method, e.g., Stir-Frying, Deep-Frying, is capitalized.

READ THE FOLLOWING BEFORE YOU START STIR-FRYING!

Preparation:

1. Read the recipe through at least once.

2. Cut the meat and vegetables into small and uniform pieces.

3. Combine ingredients in small bowls as instructed.

4. Have all the necessary ingredients and utensils on hand.

Cooking:

1. Use the highest temperature setting on your stove. If your stove is electric, preheat the burner to red-hot before using the wok.

2. Over a high flame, heat the wok until smoking. Add the oil and heat again until almost smoking. Swirl oil to coat the wok. Add food and stir vigorously and thoroughly (except soft-textured items, such as fish and bean curd, which must be stirred gently). Stirring consists of 3 motions: ① Scooping, ② Turning, and ③ Hitting with spatula to separate. The 3 motions can also be done by flipping food in a one-handed wok, if you have a strong wrist.

3. You must hear a loud noise when food is introduced into the hot oil, otherwise the oil is not hot enough.

4. Turn heat lower if food has a tendency to burn.

5. Different ingredients are often cooked in separate batches to avoid over-crowding in the wok. Cook vegetables first and set them aside, then meat, then return the vegetables to the wok for the final tossing of everything, thus avoiding cooking the meat twice, which will make it tough.

6. Don't overcook. When I say "Stir for 30 seconds," I really mean "30 seconds!" Remove food from the wok as soon as cooking is finished. Food left in the wok will continue to cook even when heat is turned off.

7. Serve most dishes as soon as they are cooked.

炒包心菜

Stir-Fried Cabbage

We start off Stir-Frying with two simple vegetables: the first one without Simmering, and the second one with Simmering. Once you master these, you can Stir-Fry any vegetable. Virtually any vegetable can be combined with any other vegetable, meat, poultry, or seafood, to make a mixed dish (see Beef and Snowpeas on p. 26, and Pork and Peppers on p. 25).

    2 tablespoons oil
    3 cloves garlic, crushed
    ½ teaspoon salt
    5 cups shredded cabbage
      a pinch of pepper

Heat oil in wok over high flame until smoking, fry garlic and salt until aromatic. Add cabbage and stir for 1 minute. Sprinkle with pepper, discard garlic. Stir once and serve, either hot or cold. You may omit garlic and sprinkle with chopped scallions before serving.

Other Applications:

Stir-Fried Bok Choy or Chinese Mustard Greens:
Substitute bok choy or Chinese mustard greens for cabbage. Separate stem from leaves. Cut into bite-sized pieces. Stir stems for ½ minute, add leaves, and stir for another ½ minute.

Stir-Fried Spinach or Bean Sprouts: Substitute ½ pound spinach or 4 cups bean sprouts for cabbage. Stir for only 20 seconds. Transfer onto serving platter immediately and let the retained heat finish off the cooking.

Stir-Fried Cabbage and Carrots: Use 4 cups shredded cabbage and 1 cup shredded carrots. Stir carrots for 1 minute, add cabbage and stir for another minute.

炒胡蘿蔔

Stir-Fried Carrots

"My son never ate cooked carrots before and now he is eating them like mad!" exclaimed one of my students.

    1 pound carrots
    2 tablespoons oil
    ½ teaspoon salt
    ½ cup broth (any kind) or water
    1 whole scallion, chopped
      a dash of pepper

Scrape carrots. ② Cut them diagonally into ⅛″ slices.

Heat oil in wok over high flame until very hot, add carrots and stir for half a minute. Add salt and broth. Turn heat to medium, cover and simmer until the desired tenderness is achieved: two minutes if you prefer it crunchy; longer, if soft. Stir occasionally while simmering.

Can be prepared ahead of time. Just before serving, sprinkle with scallion and pepper. Serve hot or cold.

Other Applications:

Stir-Fried Asparagus: Substitute 1½ pounds asparagus for carrots. Use only the tender tips. Omit scallion.

Stir-Fried Broccoli or Cauliflower: Substitute 1½ pounds broccoli or cauliflower for carrots. Separate florets from stems. Split larger florets lengthwise into bite-sized pieces. Slice stem lengthwise into 2″ pieces after peeling skin.

Dried Shrimp and Chinese Cabbage: Substitute ½ head Chinese cabbage for carrots. Cut into 1½″ sections. Split the root. Use 1 tablespoon dried shrimp, soaked in ¼ cup warm water. Drain and reserve liquid. Fry shrimp before adding cabbage. Use the reserved liquid in place of the broth above. Decrease salt.

Stir-Fried String Beans: Substitute 1 pound string beans for carrots. String.

魚香茄子

Fish-Fragrant Eggplant

There are 21 distinct flavors in Sichuan cuisine. Each is a composite of various spices prepared in different ways. The best known are Gung Bao, Peppery-Hot, Sour-Hot, Garlic Sauce, Ginger Sauce, Five-Fragrant, Odd-Flavor, and Fish-Fragrant. No matter how hard you exercise your imagination, this dish never tastes fishy. It is called "Fish-Fragrant" because the original recipe called for oil in which fish was fried.

    1 pound eggplant*
    ½ cup oil

Meat Mixture
    ¼ pound ground pork
    2 teaspoons finely chopped garlic
    2 teaspoons finely chopped
      ginger
    1 whole scallion, chopped
    1 teaspoon hot bean sauce**

Seasoning
    ¼ teaspoon salt
    ½ teaspoon sugar
    ¼ teaspoon vinegar
    1 teaspoon wine
    1 tablespoon soy sauce
    ¼ cup broth or water

    1 teaspoon cornstarch
    1 teaspoon sesame oil
    ¼ teaspoon ground Sichuan pepper

*Chinese eggplant is preferred
**Add more to taste
Peel eggplant if the skin is tough. Cut lengthwise into finger-sized strips. Assemble **Meat Mixture** and **Seasoning.**

Heat oil until hot, add eggplant. Turn heat to medium and stir intermittently until soft (about 5 minutes). ② Push to side of wok to press out excess oil with a spatula. Set eggplant aside.

Pour out all but 1 tablespoon oil. Heat until hot. Stir **Meat Mixture** until pork changes color. Add **Seasoning** and eggplant. When it boils, turn heat to medium, cover, and simmer for 1 minute. *May be prepared ahead up to this point, kept warm or refrigerated and reheated.* Thicken with cornstarch mixed with some water. Add sesame oil and Sichuan pepper.

①

②

炒八寶菜

Eight-Jewelled Vegetables

This vegetarian dish looks and tastes so meaty that it is often mistaken for a meat dish. It is so high in protein and hearty in taste that nobody will even miss the meat!

Dried Vegetables
    4 dried mushrooms
    ¼ cup dried tiger lilies
    ¼ cup wood ears

Other Vegetables
    1 carrot
    ½ cup bamboo shoots
    8 ears baby corn
    ½ cup golden needle mushrooms
    ½ cup snow peas

Seasoning
    1 teaspoon sugar
    1 tablespoon light soy sauce
    1 teaspoon sesame oil
    ¼ cup water

    1 2-oz. bundle bean threads
    2 tablespoons oil
    1 10-oz. can mock meat

Soak the **Dried Vegetables** in warm water for 30 minutes. Drain. Discard stems of mushrooms and wood ears. Quarter if large.

Scrape carrot and slice diagonally. Slice bamboo shoots. Drain baby corn and discard liquid. Cut off root ends of golden needle mushrooms. String snow peas.

Combine **Seasoning.** Soak bean threads in warm water for 5 minutes; drain and cut into 3″ sections.

Heat oil over high flame. Fry soaked **Dried Vegetables** for ½ minute. Add other vegetables in the order listed, stir after each addition. Pour in **Seasoning** and stir until liquid boils. Stir in bean threads and mock meat until heated. Serve hot or cold.

Other Applications:
Try different combinations of vegetables. For instance, in the above recipe, use just the carrots, broccoli and bamboo shoots. Call it the **Trio of Vegetables**. Always cook the vegetables that take the longest first (in this case, the carrot); then add the broccoli, followed by the bamboo shoots. Stir after each addition.

葱炒蛋

Eggs and Scallions

Who says a Chinese meal has to be complicated? If you can't think of anything else for supper tonight, try this easy and pleasing dish. Just add a Stir-Fried vegetable and a pot of hot rice, and you have supper ready! Fluffy eggs are made in a hot, uncrowded wok. Make two batches if you use more than 3 eggs. (Two batches are pictured here.)

- 2 whole scallions
- 3 eggs
- ½ teaspoon salt
- 2 tablespoons oil
- 1 tablespoon oyster sauce (optional)

Chop scallions. Mix with eggs and salt. Beat well.

Over high flame, heat oil until smoking. Swirl oil to coat wok. Add eggs. Stir quickly until set. Transfer them to serving platter. Sprinkle with oyster sauce. Serve hot.

青椒肉片

Pork and Peppers

You can Stir-Fry pork either marinated or unmarinated. The former is more tender and velvety; the latter is more flavorful. This recipe demonstrates how pork can be cooked without any marinade. Don't let its simplicity fool you; this dish is extraordinarily tasty.

- ½ pound pork butt
- 2 bell peppers

Seasoning I
- 3 cloves garlic
- 2 tablespoons fermented black beans
- 3 slices ginger
- 2 scallions
- 1 teaspoon Sichuan hot bean sauce*

Seasoning II
- 1 teaspoon sugar
- 1 teaspoon sesame oil
- 1 tablespoon dark soy sauce

- 2 tablespoons oil

*Add more to taste

Cut pork into 1" x 2" x ¼" slices. Cut peppers into diamond-shaped pieces. Crush garlic. Rinse black beans in cold water. Mince everything in **Seasoning I.** Assemble **Seasoning II** in a separate bowl.

Heat 2 tablespoons oil in wok until hot. Stir in **Seasoning I** until aromatic. Add pork and stir until color changes. Stir in peppers for 2 minutes. Add **Seasoning II** and stir. *May be prepared ahead and kept warm or re-heated.*

蠔油雪豆牛肉

Beef and Snowpeas
in Oyster Sauce

Many a student's palate has been so tickled by this exotic ingredient that there has been a run on oyster sauce in local Oriental stores.

¾ pound beef, sirloin or flank

Marinade
1 teaspoon cornstarch
1 teaspoon soy sauce
1 teaspoon wine
1 tablespoon oyster sauce

1 small onion, any kind
2 cups snowpeas
3 tablespoons oil, divided
  a few dashes of salt
2 tablespoons water
1 tablespoon soy sauce

Preparing Ahead

② Cut beef across the grain into ⅛″ slices. ③ Combine with **Marinade** and let stand for 15 minutes. ④ Chop onion coarsely. ⑤ String snowpeas and rinse. Heat wok over high flame until smoking. Add one tablespoon oil, which should be heated in seconds. Stir onion briefly (turn heat lower if it tends to burn). Add snowpeas and stir briefly. Sprinkle salt while stirring. Set aside.

Last-Minute Stir-Frying

Heat wok again over high flame until smoking. Heat the remaining 2 tablespoons oil in the wok until very hot. Stir beef in quickly, until it is almost cooked. ⑥ Add onion, snowpeas, water and soy sauce. Stir a few times and serve.

Other Applications:

Substitute other vegetables, such as green peppers and asparagus, for snowpeas.

杏仁鷄丁

Almond Chicken Dices

Students tell me that they use this recipe again and again, because it is very easy to make, delicious to eat, and delightful to look at.

    2 whole chicken breasts

Marinade
    1 teaspoon salt
    2 teaspoons cornstarch
    1 tablespoon wine
    3 slices ginger

    6 dried mushrooms
    2 tablespoons oil
    1 10-oz. package frozen peas
      (no need to thaw)
    ½ cup toasted almonds

Preparing Ahead
Skin and bone chicken breast. Cut into ½" cubes. Cubes should fill 2 cups. Combine with **Marinade** and set aside for 20 minutes.

Soak mushrooms in warm water for 20 minutes. Discard water and stems. Quarter.

Last-Minute Cooking
Heat 2 tablespoons oil in wok until very hot. Fry mushrooms for 30 seconds. Add chicken and stir until almost cooked. Add peas and toss until heated. Discard ginger. Transfer to a serving platter. Garnish with almonds. Serve hot.

Other Applications:
Chicken with Snow Peas: Cut chicken into ⅛" slices. Substitute ¼ pound of snow peas for peas. String snow peas, and blanch in fast boiling water for 1 minute. Drain. Cool in cold water and drain again. Sliced bamboo shoots can also be added when you add the snow peas. Omit almonds.

Chicken with Cucumbers: (Here is a dish for the delicate palate.) Substitute 2 cucumbers for peas. Peel, de-seed and slice. Stir-Fry in 1 tablespoon oil. Add a pinch of white pepper. Omit almonds.

腰果蝦仁

Shrimp with Cashews (Modified Restaurant-Style)

Oil-Blanching makes this dish look and taste professional — clear, bright and succulent.

¾ pound large shrimp

Marinade
¼ teaspoon salt
2 teaspoons cornstarch
½ egg white

Vegetables
2 whole scallions, chopped
2 teaspoons finely chopped ginger
½ cup water chestnuts, sliced

Seasoning
¼ teaspoon salt
1 teaspoon wine
½ teaspoon sesame oil

4 cups oil for blanching
½ cup roasted cashews

Preparing Ahead
Shell and devein shrimp. Rinse under cold water and drain. Mix with **Marinade** and let stand in the refrigerator for 30 minutes.
Combine **Vegetables** and **Seasoning** in two separate bowls.

Last-Minute Cooking
Just before serving, heat oil to hot, about 350°F. Have a strainer on hand. Oil-Blanch shrimp and stir quickly. Drain as soon as shrimp changes color. Remove all but 1 tablespoon oil from wok (save excess oil for other uses). Heat until hot. Fry **Vegetables** until aromatic. Add shrimp and **Seasoning,** stir until heated. Transfer onto serving platter. Garnish with cashews and serve hot.

Other Applications:
Shrimp and Snowpeas: Substitute 4 oz. snowpeas for cashews. String and blanch in boiling water for 1 minute. Drain and rinse in cold water. Stir with shrimp. Garnish is optional.

糟溜魚片

Fish Slices in Wine Sauce

This creamy, slightly sweet dish is very pleasing. Use strictly fresh fish, handle it gently, use not-too-hot oil for blanching. The wine rice gives it its unique flavor. You can either purchase the wine rice from the Oriental grocer, or make it at home (see p.132).

1 pound fillet of fish*

Marinade
½ teaspoon salt
2 teaspoons cornstarch
½ teaspoon wine
½ egg white

Wine Sauce
1 cup broth, seasoned with salt
1 tablespoon cornstarch
1 teaspoon sugar
2 tablespoons wine rice (p.132)

2 cups oil for blanching
3 slices ginger
2 cloves garlic, crushed

* Use any white, firm fish fillet, such as sole, cod or haddock. If you have any doubts about the freshness, use frozen fillets. Start marinating before completely thawed.

Preparing Ahead
Cut fillet along the grain into approximately ½″ x 1″ x 2″ slices. Mix gently with **Marinade** and set aside in the refrigerator for 30 minutes.

Combine **Wine Sauce** ingredients and set aside.

Have a strainer on hand. Heat 2 cups oil in wok until warm, about 300°F. (The oil should be fairly new.) Add fish slices and stir gently, until color changes. Do not let them brown. Drain and set aside.

Remove all but 2 tablespoons oil from wok. (The excess can be used again for other recipes.) Heat until hot. Stir in ginger and garlic until aromatic. Add **Wine Sauce** and stir until the liquid thickens. Return fish and toss gently until heated. Remove ginger and garlic. Serve hot.

①

①

②

宮保鷄丁

Gung Bao Chicken (Modified Restaurant-Style)

This famous dish was created by the chef of a former Gung Bao, *the tutor of the prince. Ding Gung Bao, whose real name was Ding Baojen, was a native of Gueijou Province. He later became the governor of Sichuan, and his favorite dish became a sensation of that province. The following recipe is done in modified restaurant-style.*

2 whole chicken breasts

Marinade
- 2 teaspoons cornstarch
- 1 tablespoon dark soy sauce
- 1 tablespoon wine

Seasoning
- 2 tablespoons water
- 1 teaspoon cornstarch
- ¼ teaspoon m.s.g.
- 1 tablespoon sugar
- 1 tablespoon vinegar
- 2 tablespoons dark soy sauce

- 6 cups oil for blanching
- 1 teaspoon Sichuan peppercorn
- 2 to 10 dried chilies, cut if large
- 1 teaspoon finely chopped ginger
- 2 whole scallions, cut into 1″ sections
- ½ teaspoon sesame oil
- ½ cup shelled, roasted peanuts

Preparing Ahead

Skin and bone chicken breast. Cut into ¾″ cubes. Mix with **Marinade** and let stand for 15 minutes. Assemble **Seasoning.**

Last-Minute Cooking

Have a strainer on hand. Heat oil in wok to warm, about 300°F. Add chicken and stir quickly. ② As soon as the color changes, drain and set aside.

Remove all but 2 tablespoons oil from wok. (Reserve the excess for other uses). Heat until very hot. Add peppercorn and fry until aromatic. ③ Remove as many peppercorns as you can. ④ In pepper-flavored oil, fry chilies until black. Stir in ginger and scallions. Return chicken and add **Seasoning.** Stir until heated. Sprinkle sesame oil and 1 teaspoon of oil reserved earlier. Stir once more and transfer onto serving platter. Sprinkle with peanuts and serve hot.

Other Applications:

To adapt to Family-Style Cooking: Omit m.s.g. and omit 1 teaspoon oil reserved earlier. Instead of Oil-Blanching, use ¼ cup oil and stir chicken in 2 batches.

醬爆鷄丁

Chicken in Crackling Sauce

This particular Stir-Frying method is called Jiang Bao, 醬爆, *which literally means "Crackle with bean sauce." The amount of chicken used must be small, but the amount of oil must be larger than what is customarily used for Stir-Frying; and the oil must be very hot. The resulting dish is as exciting as fire crackers on the Fourth of July!*

    1 whole chicken breast

Marinade
    1 teaspoon cornstarch
    1 tablespoon dark soy sauce
    1 teaspoon wine

Vegetables
    ½ cup diced carrots
    1 green pepper, diced
    ½ cup diced bamboo shoots

Seasoning
    1 tablespoon bean sauce
    1 teaspoon Sichuan hot bean sauce*
    1 small onion, any kind, chopped
    1 teaspoon finely chopped ginger
    1 teaspoon finely chopped garlic

    4 tablespoons oil, divided
    ¼ teaspoon salt
    ¼ cup roasted peanuts

*Add more to taste

Preparing Ahead

Skin and bone chicken breast. Dice into ½" pieces. Combine with **Marinade** and let stand for 15 minutes. Assemble **Vegetables** and **Seasoning** separately.

Heat 1 tablespoon oil in wok until hot. Stir in **Vegetables** *in the order listed.* Sprinkle with ¼ teaspoon salt. Set aside.

Heat the remaining 3 tablespoons oil in wok until very hot. Fry **Seasoning** until aromatic. Add chicken and toss until almost cooked. Return **Vegetables** to wok. Stir until heated. Transfer to a serving platter. Sprinkle with nuts. Serve hot.

京醬肉絲

Pork Shreds in Peking Sauce

This dish of pork shreds on green scallions is called Pork Shreds in Peking Sauce because it is cooked in sweet bean paste, a product of Peking. Hoisin sauce and sweet bean paste taste similar, the former being sweeter. I usually use hoisin sauce in this recipe so that I don't have to store another little jar of spice.

¾ pound lean pork

Marinade
1 teaspoon cornstarch
1 tablespoon dark soy sauce
1 tablespoon wine
1 tablespoon water

2 cups shredded scallions,
  with greens
¼ cup oil
2 tablespoons hoisin sauce
½ teaspoon sesame oil

Cut pork into ⅛″ shreds. Add **Marinade** and stir until liquid is absorbed. Let stand for 15 minutes. Line bottom of serving platter with scallions.

Heat ¼ cup oil in wok until hot, fry pork until color turns pale. ② Remove pork with slotted spoon. Leave oil in wok.

Heat oil again until hot. Turn heat to medium. Fry hoisin sauce briefly. Add meat and stir for 20 seconds. ③ Pour off excess oil. Sprinkle with sesame oil and pour over scallions. Mix the two at the table.

Other Applications
Beef Shreds in Peking Sauce: Substitute beef for pork.

葱爆羊肉

Scallioned Lamb (Top Picture)

Many Chinese eat lamb, but not beef. Some refuse to eat the meat of an animal which tills the soil for life-sustaining rice; others refrain from eating beef because they carry over into Buddhism the Hindu respect for the cow.

This recipe brings out the best in lamb, and takes away the unpleasant odor, Even people who usually do not eat lamb enjoy this recipe.

¾ pound lamb

Marinade
1 teaspoon cornstarch
1 teaspoon ground Sichuan pepper
1 tablespoon soy sauce
1 teaspoon oil

Seasoning
2 cups shredded scallions, with greens
1 tablespoon soy sauce
1 tablespoon sesame oil

3 tablespoons oil
1 tablespoon finely sliced garlic
1 stalk fresh coriander, chopped

Preparing Ahead
Slice lamb into slices as thin as possible. Combine with **Marinade.** Let stand for 15 minutes. Combine **Seasoning.**

Last-Minute Cooking
Heat oil until very hot. Fry garlic until aromatic. Add lamb and stir quickly until color changes. Add **Seasoning.** Stir for 30 seconds. Garnish with coriander and serve immediately.

Other Applications
Scallioned Beef: Substitute flank steak for lamb. Substitute a pinch of ground pepper for Sichuan pepper. Since beef is not as strong-tasting as lamb, you will want to use less garlic and sesame oil, or even omit both.

DEEP-FRYING METHOD 炸

Read this chapter before you Deep-Fry

Immersing food in hot oil until fully cooked is called *Deep-Frying*. It is different from *Oil-Blanching* which does not fully cook the food.

True Chinese Deep-Frying is also different from what one may find in some Chinese-American restaurants. They add oil to the batter to make food crunchy. Their batter-fried sweet and sour pork is different from the authentic Chinese sweet and sour pork in which the meat is not battered, but coated with a mixture of flours. For the Chinese, *Batter-Frying* is synonymous with *Soft-Frying*. One example is Sweet and Sour Fish Slices, a batter-fried fish which is soft and delicate.

The two most important factors in successful Deep-Frying are temperature and timing. If the temperature is too low or cooking time is too short, food will be soggy, oily or undercooked; if too high or too long, food will be burned or too dry.

Professional Chinese cooks use 7 different grades of hotness when Deep-Frying. However, all that we need to be able to do is to distinguish between different temperature *ranges*. Experience is the best guide. A good candy thermometer is a good investment before you gain enough experience. Or drop a cube of bread into the oil; its browning provides a crude test. You can tell the temperature ranges as follows:

Warm Below 300°F	Moderately Hot Around 325°F	Hot Around 350°F	Very Hot Above 375°F
Slow moving bubbles Brown in 2 minutes	Fast moving bubbles Brown in 1 minute	Very fast moving bubbles Brown in 30 seconds	Explosive movement Brown in 15 seconds

In actual frying, the length of time depends on several factors — the temperature and the amount of oil used, the size and the amount of food fried, the kind of food fried. The appearance of the outside may be misleading because it does not always indicate if the inside is done. To test whether food is done:

For large item, press it. If springy, it's done; if soggy, it's not.

For small pieces, open up a piece and see. If the color is even, it's done.

What kind of oil to use? Any vegetable oil except Oriental sesame oil and olive oil is fine. Oil can be used over and over again. Discard only when it is very dirty (see p.15).

What utensils to use? Any pot that can withstand high heat, such as a wok, an iron pot, an electric fryer, or just any old pot that you won't miss. I prefer the wok because with the same amount of oil, the wok provides a larger surface than a cylinder-shaped pan. Be extra careful when you fry in a wok. Use a collar so that the wok will sit securely.

Procedure for frying small items:
1. Use enough oil so that pieces can float freely. Never crowd the oil.
2. Have a pair of chopsticks (or tongs) and a strainer on hand.
3. Heat oil to proper temperature.
4. If batter is used, dip pieces in batter individually just before frying.
5. Fry in batches. Bring oil to the right temperature between batches.
6. Serve as soon as possible, otherwise Double-Fry (see below) or re-heat in a 350°F oven.

Procedure for frying large items:
1. Use enough oil so that more than half of the piece is immersed.
2. Have a medium or large strainer on hand.
3. Heat oil to proper temperature.
4. Use very hot oil 375°F to create an initial crust. The oil temperature is going to drop when the food is introduced. Try to maintain moderately hot temperature (275°F-300°F) until one side is almost done. Raise the temperature for the last minute of frying to get rid of the excess oil. Turn and repeat.
5. Serve as soon as possible, otherwise Double-Fry (see below) or re-heat in a 350°F oven.

Double-Frying: Food can be partially or fully fried in advance and set aside at room temperature, refrigerated, or frozen. Items must be brought to room temperature before re-frying. Use higher oil temperature for the second frying in order to avoid sogginess. Double-Fried food is even crispier than Single-Fried if it is done properly. Restaurants use this method to avoid the dinner-time rush. So can we.

2. DEEP-FRYING METHOD DEMONSTRATION RECIPE

百角蝦球

Many-Cornered Shrimp Balls

This is a handy recipe to have. The various applications provide you with an assortment of fried appetizers made out of this basic shrimp paste. They make a hit at every party!

Shrimp Paste
- 1 slice ginger
- 1 scallion stem, cut into sections
- ½ pound raw shrimp
- ¼ cup water chestnuts
- 1 teaspoon cornstarch
- 1 teaspoon wine
- ½ teaspoon salt
- ½ egg white

- 4 slices bread
- oil for Deep-Frying
- Salt and Pepper Dip (p.130)

Preparing Ahead

Shell, devein and rinse shrimp. Set steel blade in food processor. (May also be prepared in a blender or chopped by hand, although these methods take a lot longer.) Mince ginger. Add scallion and mince. Add shrimp and water chestnuts, chop with 2 quick on/off turns. Add rest of **Shrimp Paste** ingredients. Process with a few quick on/off turns until water chestnuts are coarsely chopped. Do not over-process.

Trim crusts and cut bread into pea-sized cubes. Spread on cookie sheet and bake in 300°F oven for 5 minutes to dry.

Shape Shimp Paste into balls by dipping hand in water to prevent sticking. ② Grab handful of mixture and squeeze out 1″ balls from top of fist. Transfer balls into bread cubes. ③ Roll them in cubes to cover. ④ Squeeze them gently to make the bread stick.

Last-Minute Cooking

Have strainer and chopsticks on hand. Heat oil to warm (275°F). Add all the balls. Raise heat to high. Fry for 3 minutes. Drain on paper towel. Serve immediately, either with Salt and Pepper Dip or alone. *See Double-Frying (p.34) to avoid last-minute rush.*

Other Applications:

Shrimp Toast: Use 8 slices bread. Trim crust and cut each into 4 quarters. Spread on cookie sheet and bake in 300°F oven for 5 minutes. Spread **Paste** on one side. Decorate with coriander leaves if desired. Fry at 375°F with shrimp side down for 1 minute. Turn over and fry for a few more seconds.

Puffed Shrimp Balls: Omit bread. Double **Shrimp Paste.** Shape into 16 balls. Fry at 375°F for 2 to 3 minutes.

魚捲
Fish Spring Rolls

Spring Rolls are wrapped in a thinner and crispier skin than egg rolls and filled with a more elaborate filling (meat, seafood, or vegetables). A mixture of meat and vegetables is used as filling in the picture on the left.

Filling
- 1 pound fillet of fish (any with white meat)
- 2 scallion stems
- 1 teaspoon salt
- 1 teaspoon wine
- 1 teaspoon sesame oil
- 1 tablespoon lard or oil
- ½ teaspoon finely chopped ginger
- 1 egg white

- 20 spring roll wrappers*
- 1 egg, beaten
  oil for Deep-Frying
  Salt and Pepper Dip (p.130)

*If not available, use egg roll wrappers or bean curd skins.

Preparing Ahead
Cut fish into pinkie-sized strips. Chop scallions finely. Combine all **Filling** ingredients.

Wrapping
Place one wrapper rough side down on the table. Place 2 fish strips and filling along the edge. ② Fold the edge over and roll half way. ③ Fold both ends toward center. ④ Smear egg along edges. Roll further and set on tray on the sealed side.

Last-Minute Cooking
Have chopsticks on hand. Heat frying oil to 350°F. Drop in the rolls, one by one, and fry until one side is brown, about 2 minutes. Turn and repeat. Drain on paper towels. Serve with Salt and Pepper Dip. See Double-Frying on p. 34 to avoid last-minute rush.

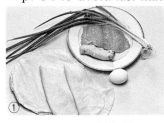

生炸子鷄
Fried Spring Chicken

Finger-licking good fried chicken in a deliciously different way! And probably a lot simpler than your familiar recipes. Remember to make the initial temperature really hot to create a crust; also the final temperature must be hot enough to get rid of the excess oil. In between, the temperature should be just hot enough to cook the chicken thoroughly. Be extra careful — the oil is hot!

1 small fryer or 2 whole chicken breasts

Marinade
- ½ teaspoon salt
- 1 tablespoon soy sauce
- 1 teaspoon wine

Garnish
- 1 tablespoon sugar
- 1 tablespoon vinegar
- 3 tablespoons light soy sauce
- 1 teaspoon sesame oil
- 1 whole scallion, chopped
- 1 tablespoon chopped fresh chili (optional)
- 1 tablespoon finely chopped ginger
- 1 tablespoon finely chopped garlic

- 2 quarts oil for Deep-Frying

Preparing Ahead
Ask the butcher to chop the chicken into bite-sized pieces, together with skin and bones. Combine with **Marinade** and toss lightly. Let stand for 20 minutes. Drain. Assemble **Garnish** ingredients.

Frying
Have a skimmer on hand. Heat oil to 375°F. Fry chicken in two batches: Carefully drop chicken pieces in, one by one. The oil temperature will drop abruptly when you add the chicken. Fry in warm oil for 3 minutes. Take out the pieces and set aside. Raise temperature to 375°F and repeat with second batch. Again raise the temperature to 375°F and fry both batches for 1 minute. Drain. Reserve the oil for other uses. Sprinkle **Garnish** over chicken. Serve hot or cold.

蘇卅燻魚

Pseudo-Smoked Fish

This ingenious dish comes from Suchow, a beautiful city in East China. The fish looks and tastes smoked, but it is not smoked! A good wine goes well with the fabulous fake smoked fish.

2 pounds of fish steaks

Marinade
3 whole scallions
3 slices ginger
½ teaspoon salt
2 tablespoons dark soy sauce
2 tablespoons light soy sauce
1 tablespoon wine

Sauce
1 cup water
¼ cup sugar
1 teaspoon five-spice powder

1 tablespoon sesame oil
oil for Deep-Frying

*Carp is preferred. If not available, use any firm fish steak.

Smash scallions and ginger with side of cleaver. Cut the former into 2″ sections. Combine with the rest of the **Marinade**, together with the fish, and let stand for 6 hours or overnight.

Drain fish and add the excess **Marinade** to **Sauce** ingredients. Bring to boil. Simmer for 5 minutes. Add sesame oil and keep warm.

Heat oil to 350°F. Have chopsticks or tongs on hand. Fry fish, one batch at a time, until dark brown, about 3 minutes. Stir frequently. Take fish pieces out and immediately dip into the **Sauce** for 1 minute. Take out and transfer to a serving platter. Continue the process with the rest. Serve cold. Can be kept in the refrigerator for weeks or frozen indefinitely.

糖醋鱼片

Sweet and Sour Fish Slices

Don't let the colorful look and delicious taste of this dish fool you! It is quite simple to make, so try it and take a bow! It is different from the crunchy and doughy dish found in some Chinese restaurants overseas.

1 pound fish fillet or steak*

Marinade
- ½ teaspoon salt
- 1 teaspoon wine
- ¼ teaspoon ginger juice
- 1 teaspoon light soy sauce

Batter
- 6 tablespoons water
- ½ cup flour
- ¼ teaspoon baking powder
- 1 egg, beaten

Sauce
- ¾ cup broth or water
- 2 tablespoons cornstarch
- 6 tablespoons sugar
- 6 tablespoons vinegar
- 4 tablespoons ketchup
- 2 tablespoons light soy sauce

- 1 tablespoon oil for Stir-Frying
- 1 small onion, coarsely chopped
- 1 carrot, diced

- ½ cup frozen peas
  oil for Deep-Frying

* Any fish with firm, white meat: either fresh, or newly thawed.

Preparing Ahead
Cut fish into large slices, about ⅓″ thick. Combine with **Marinade** and let stand for 15 minutes. Combine **Batter** ingredients and mix into a thin **Batter**. Assemble **Sauce** ingredients.

Heat 1 tablespoon oil in saucepan until hot. Add onion and carrot. Stir for 1 minute. Stir in **Sauce** ingredients until thickened. Keep warm. Add peas just before serving.

Last-Minute Cooking
Bring oil to hot (350°F). Dip fish fillet in **Batter,** one piece at a time; shake off excess and drop into oil. Fry one side until slightly brown, about 1 minute. Turn and repeat. Drain on paper towel. Arrange on platter, pour **Sauce** over and serve hot.

咕嚕肉

Sweet and Sour Pork

Different regions in China make different kinds of Sweet and Sour Pork. The Northerners usually use just sugar and vinegar. The Easterners like to add ketchup. The Cantonese add pickles and even fruit. But if you are offered Sweet and Sour Pork in a Sichuan or Hunan restaurant, that is out of character for those regions: they don't have a sweet tooth.

1 pound pork, preferably butt

Marinade	**Sauce**
½ teaspoon salt	½ cup water
1 tablespoon flour	1 tablespoon cornstarch
1 teaspoon wine	
1 egg yolk	3 tablespoons sugar
	3 tablespoons vinegar
Coating	1 tablespoon light soy sauce
5 tablespoons cornstarch	
2 tablespoons flour	3 tablespoons ketchup
	¼ cup pickle juice

3 cloves garlic	
3 slices ginger	1 tablespoon oil for Stir-Frying
1 bell pepper	
1 cup Cantonese Pickles*	oil for Deep-Frying

* You may either make them yourself (p.117) or buy a jar of sweet pickles from the supermarket.

Use ½ cup sweet pickles and ½ cup sliced carrots.

Preparing Ahead
Trim fat and cut pork into ¾" cubes. Combine with **Marinade** and let stand for 15 minutes. Roll pieces in **Coating.** Squeeze into balls.

Crush garlic. Slice pepper and pickles. Mix **Sauce** ingredients.

Heat 1 tablespoon oil in saucepan. Add garlic and ginger, stir until aromatic. Stir in pepper and pickles. Pour in **Sauce** ingredients. Stir until thickened. Keep warm.

Last-Minute Cooking
Have a strainer on hand. Heat frying oil to 350°F. Add pork and fry for 5 minutes.** Open a piece to make sure that the center is not pink. Place on serving platter. Pour **Sauce** over and serve hot.

** Use Double-Frying method to avoid last-minute hassle, see p. 34.

糖醋菠蘿排骨

Sweet and Sour Pineapple Spareribs

Colorful, tasty and crisp, this dish is always a hit! You can use the following recipe to make a main dish. For an appetizer, use Salt and Pepper Spareribs (see below).

    2-3 pounds small pork ribs
    2 tablespoons dark soy sauce
    2 cloves garlic
    1 green pepper
    1 tomato

Sauce
    ½ cup water
    2 tablespoons cornstarch
    2 tablespoons sugar
    3 tablespoons vinegar
    1 tablespoon dark soy sauce
    ½ cup juice from canned pineapple
      chunks
    _____
    1 tablespoon oil for stirring
    oil for frying
    ½ cup canned pineapple chunks

Preparing Ahead
Ask the butcher to cut across the bones into three strips, then separate the ribs. Boil them in a large pot of boiling water until no more pink juice comes out when pierced with a fork, about 20 minutes. Drain and marinate with 2 tablespoons dark soy sauce for 20 minutes. Spread out on tray to dry. About 1 hour.

Smash and peel garlic. Cut pepper into 1" squares. Cut tomato into chunks. Assemble **Sauce** ingredients.

Heat 1 tablespoon oil in saucepan. Add garlic and stir until aromatic. Stir in pepper. Add **Sauce** ingredients and stir until thickened. Add tomato and pineapple. Keep warm.

Last-Minute Cooking
Have a skimmer on hand. Heat frying oil to 350°F. Fry ribs until brown, about 1 minute. Transfer to serving platter. Pour **Sauce** over ribs and serve hot.

Other Applications
Salt and Pepper Spareribs: Substitute **Salt and Pepper Dip** (see p.130) for the above **Sauce**. Set the **Dip** on the side of serving platter. Use as a main dish or an appetizer.

Sweet and Sour Spareribs: Substitute **Sauce** in **Sweet and Sour Pork** (see p.40) for the above **Sauce**.

檸檬鷄

Lemon Chicken

This contemporary dish is becoming a classic. I would recommend the following Double-Frying method to cut down the last-minute hassle. Although restaurants slice chicken before frying, you can first fry it in large pieces and then cut it into strips.

2 whole chicken breasts

Marinade
1 tablespoon cornstarch
½ teaspoon salt
¼ teaspoon pepper
1 tablespoon light soy sauce
1 teaspoon wine
1 teaspoon sesame oil
1 egg yolk

½ cup cornstarch
¼ cup flour
6 cups oil

Sauce
½ cup broth or water
1 tablespoon cornstarch
1 teaspoon salt
6 tablespoons sugar
½ cup lemon juice

Garnish
lemon twists
fresh coriander

Preparing Ahead

Skin and bone chicken breasts. ② Slice each piece laterally into two thin slices. Combine with **Marinade**. Let stand for 20 minutes. Shake off excess. Roll each piece in cornstarch and flour mixture.

Heat oil to 300°F. Deep-Fry chicken for 2 to 3 minutes. Drain and set aside to cool.

Assemble **Sauce** in a small pan and bring it to boil over medium flame, stirring constantly. The **Sauce** will become translucent. Keep warm.

Last-Minute Cooking

Heat oil to 375°F. Return chicken and fry for 1 minute. Drain on paper towel. ③ Cut across into ½" strips. Arrange on platter and pour **Sauce** over. Decorate with **Garnish**.

宮保蝦

Gung Bao Shrimp

Only frozen, or previously frozen, shrimp is found in most American stores. If you cook it as soon as it is thawed, it tastes fine. Buy only shrimp which is frozen in shells. Shelled frozen shrimp loses most of its flavor.

1 pound raw shrimp

Marinade
½ teaspoon salt
1 teaspoon wine
1 egg yolk

Sauce
¾ cup water
2 teaspoons cornstarch
2 tablespoons brown sugar
1 tablespoon vinegar
1 tablespoon dark soy sauce

2 tablespoons oil for stirring
3 dried chilies, cut across if large
1 teaspoon chopped garlic
1 teaspoon finely chopped ginger
4 water chestnuts, sliced
oil for Deep-Frying
¼ cup cornstarch for coating

Preparing Ahead

Shell, devein and rinse shrimp. Combine with the **Marinade** and let stand for 30 minutes. Combine **Sauce** ingredients.

Heat 2 tablespoons oil in wok until hot. Add chilies and fry until black. Add garlic, ginger and water chestnuts; stir until fragrant. Add **Sauce**. When thickened, set aside and keep warm.

Last-Minute Cooking

Heat frying oil to 350°F. Have a strainer on hand. Drain shrimp and coat with cornstarch. Deep-Fry until brown, about 2 minutes. Drain on paper towel. Transfer onto serving platter. Pour **Sauce** over and serve hot.

糖衣核桃

Candied Walnut

*The Chinese have few sweets. This one has
wide appeal. In addition, unlike most Chinese
sweets, it can be prepared ahead of time and
stored for weeks.*

    1 quart water
    ½ pound walnuts
    1 teaspoon salt

Syrup
    1 cup sugar
    ½ teaspoon salt
    1 cup water

    oil for Deep-Frying

Bring 1 quart water to boil. Add walnuts and salt
and blanch for 1 minute. Drain and rinse in cold
water. Pick and pull off the darkest part of the
skin. Rinse again and drain.

Bring **Syrup** ingredients to boil. Turn heat low
and simmer about 10 minutes, or until it drops
slowly when lifted with a spoon. Add walnuts
and continue simmering for another 6 minutes.
Drain.

Heat oil to warm (about 250°F). The oil must
be fresh. Fry walnuts until medium brown,
about 3 minutes. Stir while frying. Remove
walnuts. Raise the oil temperature to 350°F.
Return walnuts and fry for another ½ minute.
Drain and spread on kitchen towel to cool. Can
store in a tightly closed jar for weeks.

SHALLOW-FRYING METHOD 煎

Shallow-Frying is cooking in a small amount of oil over medium heat, usually in a flat pan. It is slower than Stir-Frying and requires much less oil than Deep-Frying. Although it is less dramatic than the other two methods, it is easier. Since timing is less crucial, Shallow-Fried dishes can usually be prepared ahead of time and kept warm in an oven for some time.

In Shallow-Frying, food is browned on both sides, such as in Shallow-Fried Fish Slices. It is different from *Sticking,* 貼 , in which only one side is browned, thus making the top soft and moist, and the bottom crisp and crunchy, like *Guotieh. Pan-Roasting,* 烘 , is baking on top of the stove in a pan, either greased, as in Shrimp Omelet, or ungreased, as in Thin Cakes.

Shallow-Frying can be used as a single method recipe or in combination with other cooking methods. For instance, Sweet and Sour Spareribs is a combination of Shallow-Frying and Stewing. Other dishes are Shallow-Fried first, followed by *Splashing, Thickening* and *Vinegaring* (p.129).

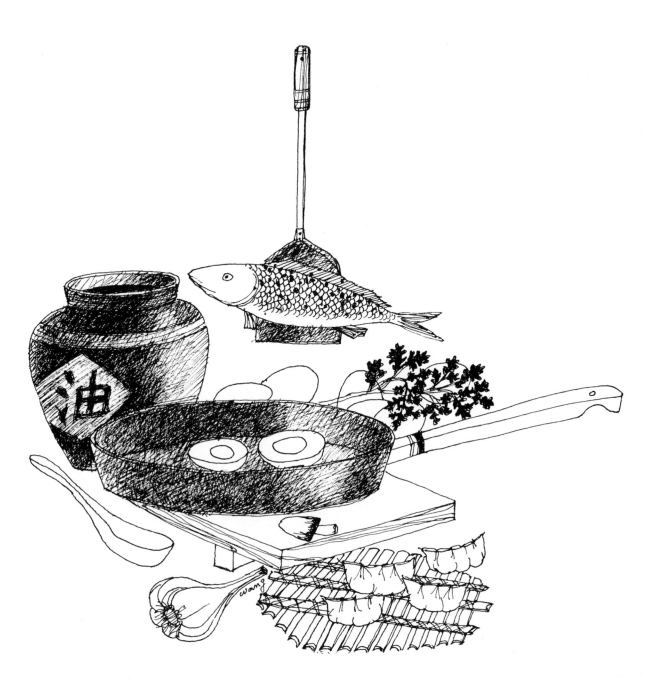

亨 蛋

Splashed Eggs

This dish is ridiculously easy and fool-proof, yet yum-yum good!

8 hard-boiled eggs

Sauce
½ teaspoon salt
1 teaspoon finely chopped ginger
1 teaspoon finely chopped garlic
1 whole scallion, finely chopped
2 teaspoons sugar
2 tablespoons soy sauce
1 tablespoon vinegar
1 tablespoon wine
1 teaspoon sesame oil (optional)

2 tablespoons oil

Peel eggs and split into halves. Assemble **Sauce** ingredients.

Heat 2 tablespoons oil in frying pan until hot. Turn heat to medium. Tilt the pan to distribute oil. ② Place eggs, cut side down, and fry until brown. Turn and repeat. ③ Splash with **Sauce**. Serve hot or cold.

煎 豬 扒

Pork Cutlet in Hoisin Sauce

If you like to serve Chinese food with knife and fork, this is a good dish to use, easy to make and delicious to eat. If you prefer to eat it with chopsticks, slice the meat after cooking.

1 pound tenderloin or 1″ thick pork chops

Marinade
½ teaspoon salt
¼ teaspoon pepper
1 tablespoon cornstarch
1 teaspoon wine
1 tablespoon light soy sauce
1 teaspoon sesame oil (optional)

Sauce
1 tablespoon hoisin sauce
1 tablespoon light soy sauce
2 tablespoons ketchup
6 tablespoons broth or water

2 tablespoons oil
3 slices ginger
2 whole scallions, cut into 2″ sections

② Cut tenderloin across grain into ½″ slices. Combine with **Marinade**. Let stand for 15 minutes. Assemble **Sauce**.

Heat 2 tablespoons oil in frying pan. Over medium heat, fry pork until color changes. ③ Turn and repeat. Set aside. Leave oil in pan.

Heat pan again and stir ginger and scallions for ½ minute. ④ Add **Sauce** ingredients and pork. Cover and simmer over medium heat for 5 minutes. Turn occasionally. Discard ginger and serve hot. *May be kept warm, refrigerated, or frozen and re-heated.*

牛爬樹
Cattle Climbing on Trees

This is a dish for those who love Chinese food but cannot give up eating a lot of meat. Large, brown slices of beef on green Chinese broccoli look great and taste delicious. If you happen to be a "strict non-vegetarian," you may want to omit the broccoli and double the rest of the ingredients in this recipe.

 1 pound sirloin or chuck

Marinade
 ½ teaspoon garlic powder
 ¼ teaspoon pepper
 a pinch of five-spice powder (optional)
 1 teaspoon cornstarch
 1 tablespoon soy sauce
 1 tablespoon wine

Sauce
 ½ cup water
 2 teaspoons cornstarch
 1 tablespoon oyster sauce
 1 tablespoon ketchup
 1 tablespoon soy sauce

 ½ pound Chinese broccoli
 2 tablespoons oil

Preparing Ahead
② Slice beef against the grain into large, ½″ slices. Combine with **Marinade** and let stand for 1 hour. Assemble **Sauce** ingredients.

③ Wash broccoli and peel stems. Drop into a large pot of boiling water. Drain after two minutes. Rinse in cold water to cool. Squeeze out excess water. Arrange broccoli in one direction on platter; cut across twice.

Last-Minute Cooking
Heat 2 tablespoons oil in frying pan or wok until hot. Fry beef, a single layer at a time, less than 1 minute on each side. Arrange pieces over broccoli. Add **Sauce** ingredients to the oil left in the pan. Heat until thickens. ④ Pour over beef and serve hot.

川味豆魚
Sichuan Bean Sprout Fish Rolls

Makes 24 rolls
Chinese vegetarians like to make vegetable dishes taste like meat, fish, chicken, abalone, goose, etc. Whether or not it tastes like fish, this is certainly a delicious dish. I like to include it in my menu because it can be served cold — no last-minute rush!

 1 pound bean sprouts
 ½ teaspoon salt
 ¼ teaspoon pepper
 a pinch m.s.g.(optional)
 8 pieces large bean curd skin
 2 tablespoons oil

Garnish
 ¼ teaspoon ground Sichuan pepper
 ½ teaspoon sugar
 1 tablespoon light soy sauce
 2 tablespoons thick soy sauce
 1 teaspoon vinegar
 1 tablespoon chili oil (optional)
 1 fresh coriander, chopped (optional)

Bring a large pot of water to boil. Drop bean sprouts in and drain immediately. Rinse in cold water to cool. Toss lightly with salt, pepper and m.s.g.

② Wrap bean curd skin in a damp, but not wet, dish towel for 10 minutes. Trim edges. Cut each piece into thirds. ③ Place bean sprouts along the round edge. Roll tightly half way. Fold both ends toward center. ④ Dab water along edges. Roll tightly the remaining half.

Heat oil in frying pan until hot. Turn heat to low and place rolls in pan, with sides touching. Fry until light brown. Take care not to burn them. Turn and repeat. When cool, cut into 1 ½″ sections and arrange on a platter. *May be refrigerated.* Combine **Garnish** and pour over rolls when ready to serve. Serve cold.

①

②

④

①

③

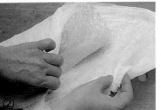
②

④

煎魚片

Shallow-Fried Fish Slices

This dish is a perennial favorite of my guests. They find it hard to believe that it is so easy to make. An additional advantage is that there is no last-minute rush.

> 1 pound fish steak or fillet of fish*
> 1 teaspoon salt

Garnish
> 1 teaspoon finely chopped ginger
> 1 teaspoon finely chopped garlic
> 1 whole scallion, chopped
> 2 tablespoons sugar
> 2 tablespoons light soy sauce
> 2 tablespoons vinegar
> 1 tablespoon broth or water
> 1 teaspoon sesame oil (optional)

> ½ cup flour
> 2 tablespoons oil

* Use any firm, white fish steak or fillet, preferably ½″ thick. Unless very fresh fish is available, use barely thawed frozen fish.

Rub fish slice with salt on both sides as soon as you bring it back from the store (or before it is completely thawed if frozen fillet is used). Leave in refrigerator for at least 1 hour. Assemble **Garnish** ingredients.

Rinse fish in cold water. ② Pat dry with paper towel. Put flour in a paper bag and shake fish slices in it, one piece at a time. Shake off excess flour.

Heat 2 tablespoons oil in frying pan until hot. ③ Over medium heat, fry fish until one side is browned, about 3 minutes. Turn and repeat. Transfer to a serving platter.
④ Pour **Garnish** over. Serve hot or cold.

鑲豆腐
Stuffed Bean Curd

Makes about 24 pieces

Don't let the pungent smell of dried shrimp turn you off! When cooked with other things, it makes each dish uniquely delicious, as described by the Chinese word: shian, 鮮 (no corresponding English expression). This word is used to describe seafood, certain types of wild game, and fresh fish and poultry. Try dried shrimp with Chinese cabbage, too (p.21).

    1 pound firm bean curd

Stuffing
    1 tablespoon dried shrimp
    1 tablespoon warm water
    1 whole scallion
    4 water chestnuts
    ¼ pound ground pork
    ¼ teaspoon ginger juice
    ½ teaspoon sesame oil (optional)

    2 tablespoons oil
    ½ teaspoon salt
    1 cup broth, seasoned with salt
    2 tablespoons dark soy sauce
    1 teaspoon cornstarch
    1 whole scallion, chopped

Cut bean curd into squares, about 2½" x 2½" x 1". ② Cut each into 2 triangles. ③ With a small knife, make a slit ¼" along the long side. ④ Carve the center out. Scrape with a teaspoon.

Soak dried shrimp in warm water for 10 minutes. Drain and reserve liquid. Mince shrimp together with scallion and water chestnuts. Mix with the rest of **Stuffing** and reserved liquid. ⑤ Use it to fill the pockets of bean curd. Heat 2 tablespoons oil in frying pan, preferably the non-stick type. ⑥ Over medium heat, stand the triangles with the opened side down in oil. Fry until light brown, sprinkling with ½ teaspoon salt. Turn and brown the two broad sides also. Add broth and soy sauce. When it boils again, turn heat low and simmer for 3 minutes. *May be prepared ahead up to this point, kept warm or refrigerated and re-heated, but not frozen.* Transfer bean curd onto serving platter. Leave liquid in pan. Thicken with cornstarch mixed with some water. Pour over bean curd. Garnish with scallions.

Other Applications
Bean Curd Stuffed with Shrimp: Substitute 6 oz. raw shrimp for pork. Shell, devein and rinse. Omit dried shrimp and add a dash of salt.

葱油餅

Scallion Cakes

Makes 4 cakes

Several recipes call for scallion stems, leaving the leaves unused. Here you have an opportunity to use the leaves creatively. The layers of crispy dough are highlighted with the scallions. If the scallions ooze out of the dough when you roll it, don't worry, it will improve the looks of the finished product.

    1 recipe Scalded Dough (p.130)
    1 teaspoon salt
      some oil or lard*
    1 cup chopped scallions, mostly green part
      oil for Shallow-Frying

* The oil makes the cake light; and the lard makes it crisp.

Divide dough into 4 portions. Shape one into a ball. Press down into a disc. Roll into a 10″ circle. ① Brush with oil or lard all over the surface; smear ¼ teaspoon salt evenly; sprinkle with ¼ cup scallions. Roll up like a scroll. Stretch gently. ② Coil into another disc. ③ Tuck ends under. ④ Flatten with palm and roll out into a 4″ cake.

Can be frozen for weeks or kept between waxed paper in the refrigerator for hours. Before serving, heat a thin layer of oil in frying pan over medium flame. Fry cakes until both sides are browned, about 10 to 12 minutes. Turn occasionally while frying. *Slow frying makes the cakes crispy.* Quarter and serve hot. *Can be kept warm or reheated, but the freshly fried are the best.*

牛肉餡餅

Beef-Filled Bing

Makes 20 patties

Bing, 餅 ,is anything made in the shape of a patty, which may be sweet or savory. Beef-filled Bing is a dish for Chinese Moslems who do not eat pork. It used to take them hours to make the filling by alternately weighing the beef down with a slab of ice and chopping. With the excellent beef available in the States, the filling can be made in a few minutes. Use this dish as a snack or an appetizer.

Filling
    1 pound ground beef
    ½ teaspoon salt
    2 tablespoons soy sauce
    1 teaspoon sesame oil
    2 scallion stems
      a pinch of pepper

    1 recipe Scalded Dough (p.130)
    2 tablespoons oil
      vinegar
      light soy sauce

Mix **Filling** thoroughly. Refrigerate for 4 hours. Divide into 20 portions.

Divide dough also into 20 portions. Shape each into a ball. Press down into a circle. ② With a rolling pin, roll into a larger circle 4½″ across. You may roll with one hand, and rotate with the other, so that the edge is thinner than the center. Separate circles with waxed paper. Place one portion of **Filling** on a circle. ③ Gather along the edge. Pinch to seal. ④ Press into a 2½″ patty. *May be kept separated by waxed paper at room temperature for a short while, or refrigerated for a few hours, or frozen for days.*

Before serving, heat 2 tablespoons oil in frying pan. Turn heat to medium. Fry *Bing* until both sides are brown, about 4 minutes (6 if frozen) Turn occasionally. Serve with vinegar and soy sauce.

薄 餅
Thin Cakes

Makes 16 cakes
Students in my cooking class have fun flipping the thin cakes. Their eyes pop open twice: first, when bubbles appear between the two cakes, and second, when the two thin cakes are successfully separated. Try it, and you will have fun!

      1 recipe Scalded Dough (p.130)
        flour
        oil

Work with half the dough, leaving the other half covered. Roll dough into a cylinder. Cut into eight pieces, rotating the cylinder after each cut. Sprinkle lightly with flour. Shape into round discs. Flatten each piece. ① Brush oil on one disc. Place another disc on top. ② With a rolling pin, roll into a 6 to 7-inch circle, rotating often and turning over occasionally.

Over medium heat, heat a frying pan until medium hot. Bake a set of cakes in the ungreased pan until bubbles appear. ③ Turn over and heat the other side. Transfer onto a plate. ④ When cooled enough to handle but still warm, pull cakes apart. Fold each into quarters. Cover with dry cloth. Learn to bake and roll at the same time. When all cakes are baked, wrap in plastic wrap. Refrigerate or freeze. Steam for 15 minutes before serving.

蝦 仁 烘 蛋
Shrimp Omelet

A little bit of shrimp really goes a long way! For best results, use shrimp frozen in shell. The additional effort in shelling is well worth the good flavor, which is absent in the shelled variety.

6 oz. raw shrimp

Marinade
¼ teaspoon salt
½ teaspoon cornstarch
1 teaspoon wine
  a pinch of pepper

Sauce
½ cup broth
1 teaspoon cornstarch
1 tablespoon dark soy
  sauce
½ teaspoon sesame oil
  (optional)

Egg Mixture
1 teaspoon flour
1 teaspoon water
4 eggs
¼ teaspoon salt

1 cup bean sprouts
1 whole scallion,
  chopped
3 tablespoons oil,
  divided

Preparing Ahead
Shell and devein shrimp. Combine with **Marinade** and let stand for 10 minutes. Assemble **Sauce**. Make **Egg Mixture** by mixing flour with water, adding eggs and salt, and beating until foamy. Rinse bean sprouts.

Heat 1 tablespoon oil in wok until hot. Stir shrimp until color changes. Add bean sprouts and scallions. Stir for ½ minute. Do not overcook. Set on a plate to cool. Drain liquid and add it to **Sauce** ingredients. Heat **Sauce** until it thickens. Keep warm.

Last-Minute Cooking
Just before serving, heat remaining 2 tablespoons oil in wok until hot. Tilt to distribute. Add eggs and tilt again. Turn heat low. When partially set, spread shrimp mixture on it, cover for 1 to 2 minutes until eggs are set. Turn and cover for another minute. Transfer onto a serving platter. Pour **Sauce** over and serve hot.

Other Applications
Pork, Beef or Crab Omelet: Substitute pork, beef or crabmeat, (fresh or canned), for shrimp.

鍋 貼
Guotieh — Pot-Stickers

Makes 36 dumplings

Once upon a time, a chef was making Jiaotze for the king. He accidentally burned the bottom of the Jiaotze. The honest chef did not seek to hide his mistake, but turned the Jiaotze upside-down, so that the king himself could see what had happened. The king took a bite, and was pleased with the dumpling. When the king asked the chef what he called it, he said: "Stuck-to-the-pot." Even though they are called "Pot-Stickers," they should not really be stuck to the pot. A well-seasoned iron skillet or a non-stick pan should do a good job of making non-sticky pot-stickers.

1 recipe Scalded Dough* (p.130)

Filling
1 10-oz. package frozen chopped spinach
1 pound ground pork (2 cups)
¼ teaspoon salt
⅛ teaspoon ground pepper
2 tablespoons soy sauce
1 teaspoon sesame oil
2 scallion stems, chopped

Dip
light soy sauce
vinegar
chili oil
sesame oil

2 tablespoons oil

* Substitute 1 pound ready-made *Jiaotze* wrappers.

Defrost spinach. Squeeze out excess liquid. Mix with the rest of the **Filling** and set aside. Make the wrapper as follows: Work with half the dough, leaving the other half covered. Roll it into a cylinder. ① Cut into 18 pieces, rotating after each cut. Sprinkle with flour. Shape into circles. Flatten. ② With a rolling pin, roll along the edge of the circle with one hand, and rotate with the other, so that the edge is thinner than the center. Separate wrappers with waxed paper. Place one heaping tablespoon **Filling** on a wrapper. ③ Fold and pinch at the mid-point. ④ Make 2 pleats on both sides of this mid-point. Pinch. Repeat with the other half.

Heat 2 tablespoons oil in skillet until hot. Turn heat to medium. Arrange *Guotieh* into rows in the skillet, with sides touching. ⑤ Fry until bottom turns crusty. Pour in ½ cup water. Cover and simmer until liquid is absorbed, about 6 minutes. Transfer onto platter with bottom side up. Serve with **Dip**.

STEWING METHOD 燒

Stewing is slowly simmering food in liquid in a closed pot until the food is tender. The pot can be a heavy saucepan, a casserole dish or a sand pot.

Stewing has several advantages. The food may be cooked ahead of time and served cold or reheated. The recipe can be doubled or tripled, or multiplied any number of times. The stewing pieces can be bite-sized chunks or even whole pieces.

With all these advantages to recommend it, why is Chinese Stewing practically unknown in the West? It is too simple! Its utter simplicity denies restaurant chefs the opportunity to show off their culinary powers. Furthermore, other methods, such as Stir-Frying and Deep-Frying, are fast, allowing you to serve many guests in a short time.

There are many methods of Stewing; there are even more terms used to describe these methods. The most popular methods of Stewing are as follows:

Red-Cooking, 紅燒 , the most often used method in the Chinese kitchen, is also the easiest. Food is slowly simmered in dark soy sauce, which makes the dish reddish-brown, not red. However, it is called red because it is a lucky color. The New Year obligatory gift of money is in red envelopes. Brides in ancient China wore red. The Ministry of Economic Affairs issues lights to characterize the state of the economy each month, the top performance being indicated by the red light.

While a larger quantity of liquid is necessary to stew over Chinese stoves because the temperature is not well-controlled, just a minimum of liquid is adequate for the American stoves. With less liquid, the flavor is not boiled away.

Smothering, 燜 , is slow-simmering in a pot with a tight-fitting lid which is not opened during the Simmering process. If you are dying to see what is going on inside, you can take a quick peek, but only one peek!

Perpetual Saucing, Lu, 滷 , is stewing food in a master sauce, or *Lu,* which is used again and again. Compared with red-cooked dishes, *Lu* dishes are stronger in flavor and firmer in texture. So red-cooked dishes are used in the main part of the dinner, and *Lu* dishes as appetizers. *Lu* eggs and meat make good sandwiches for the office or the picnic. Vegetables can beadded to red-cooked dishes, but not to *Lu* dishes.

When dark soy sauce is used in *Lu,* it is called *Red Lu.* The Cantonese make a white *Lu,* using salt instead of soy sauce. It is used to cook poultry.

Use any *Lu* recipe as a starter. Strain the sauce afterwards and keep it for subsequent *Lu* dishes. You can cook pork, beef, chicken, duck, hard-boiled eggs and mild-flavored organ meats in *Lu.* Never use seafood, rice, noodles, or vegetables in the sauce.

When re-using the master sauce to cook a new dish, don't be concerned about adding the proper amount of spices. If the food tastes strong, good; that is the way it should taste. If not strong enough, you can always add some more spices toward the end.

Keep your jar of master sauce in the refrigerator forever. Boil it once every month unless you use it more often. Add more spices each time it is used. Add liquid as needed. Give a jar of *Lu* to a friend as a house-warming gift—with a good cookbook, of course!

Clear-Simmering, Dun, 燉 , is immersing food, either a large piece as a whole, or cut up into small pieces, in boiling liquid. Just when it is about to boil again, the heat is turned low, the pot is covered and the food is simmered until tender. Only an occasional bubble should surface. The plain broth used in many soups is made this way.

Often a long process of Steaming is also referred to as *Dun.* But, to avoid confusion, cooking food by the heat of steam will be referred to as Steaming (see p.92).

Although both *Steeping* and *Clear-Simmering* involve slowly cooking food immersed in liquid, they do differ. In *Steeping,* the solid is consumed and the liquid is either discarded (Westlake Vinegar Fish), or used over and over again (Soy Sauce Chicken). In *Clear-Simmering* the liquid is consumed with the soup.

4. STEWING METHOD DEMONSTRATION RECIPES

淮牛肉

Lu Beef

Lu *is a Chinese sauce that is used again and again. Heirs battling over a pot of* lu *may sound incredible, but when it is what made the family famous, it is understandable. The never-ending stream of meat and spices over the decades lets all the aroma and flavor sink in, as the* lu *assumes a distinctive personality of its own. You will do well to start your* lu *(master sauce) with beef, because beef gives flavor, unlike eggs which tend to absorb it. In time, your* lu *can develop its own distinctive personality, and if you don't want your heirs to go to court to get custody of the pot, you may write its disposition into your will, preferably in Chinese!*

    2 pounds shank or chuck

Sauce
    ½ cup dark soy sauce
    ¼ cup wine
    2 cups water
    4 whole scallions
    4 thick slices ginger
    2 star anise

Optional
    1 teaspoon Sichuan peppercorn
    8 whole cloves
    1 Chinese cinnamon
    1 teaspoon fennel
    1 piece dried orange peel
    2 dried chili peppers
    2 cloves garlic

    2 tablespoons rock candy or sugar
    1 teaspoon sesame oil

Sew **Optional** ingredients of your choice, together with star anise, in a cloth bag. Place it with beef and **Sauce** ingredients in a heavy pot. Bring it to boil, cover and simmer over low heat for one hour. Turn occasionally. Add rock candy and continue simmering for another ½ hour.

Transfer the beef to a cutting board. Let cool. Slice it against the grain into large, thin slices. Strain the sauce. Use a portion of it and mix with sesame oil to sprinkle over the meat slices. Serve cold. Keep the excess *lu* in a jar for other *lu* dishes. It can be refrigerated for weeks or frozen indefinitely.

Other Applications:
Use pork, chicken, duck, liver, heart, hard-boiled eggs, etc. to make various *lu* dishes. If you have already started the *lu*, you only need to add a portion of the above ingredients to the *lu* when you cook a new dish.

红烧筍豆

Soy Beans with Bamboo Shoots

During the Three Kingdoms Period (220 — 265 A.D.), there was a king who had a very talented son, Tsao Jyr. The older, less talented brother was quite envious of his younger brother, and challenged him to compose a poem in the time it takes to walk seven steps, on the decidedly uninspiring subject of the pot of beans which was cooking over burning bean stalks in the kitchen. The younger brother rose to the occasion with the well-known seven-step poem:

> *The bean stalk is burning hot*
> *While the beans are weeping in the pot*
> *Aren't we from the same root*
> *Why must we be stewed so fast?*

If you like soy beans, you will love this recipe!

    12 ounces fresh, shelled soy beans*
    1 15-oz. can bamboo shoots

Seasoning
    1 tablespoon brown sugar
    1 tablespoon light soy sauce
    1 tablespoon dark soy sauce
    1 star anise
    2 whole scallions
    3 slices ginger
    1 cup water

    1 teaspoon sesame oil

*When fresh soy beans are not available, use 1 cup dried soy beans. Soak in cold water for 2 hours. Drain. Simmer in 1½ cups water until tender. Omit water in **Seasoning** and cook as below.

Rub soy beans to remove membrane. Rinse in water. Drain. Shred bamboo shoots.

Bring **Seasoning** to boil. Add soy beans and bamboo shoots. When it boils again, turn heat low, cover and simmer for ½ hour. Sprinkle with sesame oil. Serve hot or cold.

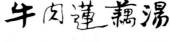

Red-Cooked Pork (Bottom Picture)

Red-Cooked Pork is as Chinese as Apple Pie is American. However, it is much easier to make. When a Chinese lady tells you "I can only Red-Cook," she means she doesn't know how to cook — because ANYBODY can Red-Cook! If the lady protesting that she can only Red-Cook overwhelms you with a fabulous banquet, don't think that she has lied to you. She is being very Chinese, and very modest!

    2 pounds pork*
    1 bamboo shoot (optional)

Seasoning
    2 whole scallions
    3 slices ginger
    3 tablespoons dark soy sauce
    1 tablespoon wine
    ½ cup water

    1 teaspoon sugar
    1 stalk fresh coriander or
      whole scallion, chopped

*Use fresh pork with some fat, such as butt.

Have the butcher cube the pork into stewing pieces or leave it whole. Roll-cut bamboo shoot (p. 9). Place **Seasoning** in a heavy saucepan.** Bring to boil, add pork, cover, turn heat low and simmer for ½ hour. Turn occasionally. Add sugar and bamboo shoots, continue to cook for another ½ hour.

Discard ginger and scallions. Garnish with coriander. Serve hot or cold.

Can be refrigerated or frozen. Cabbage, carrots, potatoes, icicle radishes, hardboiled eggs, etc. can also be added in the last half-hour of cooking.

**This can also be cooked in a casserole and served directly from it.

Other Applications:
Red-Cooked Beef: Substitute 2 pounds chuck for pork.

Beef and Lotus Root Soup

Lotus is a symbol of purity. The pure white blossoms spring out of the plant growing in muddy water. Rich in symbolism, the lotus is rich in uses too: the roots are Stewed or Stir-Fried; leaves are used to wrap food to be steamed; and the seeds are used in sweet dishes.

    1 pound lotus root
    1 pound shank or chuck
    6 cups water
    ½ teaspoon salt
    1 tablespoon dark soy sauce
    2 tablespoons wine
    1 star anise
    3 slices ginger
    1 whole scallion

Garnish
    1 stalk fresh coriander or 1 whole
      scallion, chopped
      a few drops of vinegar

Peel lotus root. ② Cube lotus root and beef. Bring 6 cups water to boil. Add everything except **Garnish**. When it boils again, turn heat low, cover and simmer until tender, about 2 hours. Discard ginger and scallion. Salt to taste. *May be prepared ahead up to this point, refrigerated and reheated.* Garnish and serve hot.

Other Applications:
Beef and Carrot Soup: Substitute carrots for lotus root. Cook beef for 1½ hours. Add carrots. Cook for ½ hour more.

川味牛腩

Sichuan Beef

It is said that a Chinese cooking a French dish makes it the best in the world. Naturally, the Chinese accent (not the m.s.g.) will enhance the original French endowments. In all fairness, the French could not be blamed if they retorted with an equally chauvinistic comment; after all, Chauvin was a fanatical French patriot. Turning from national rivalries to culinary delights, this Sichuan dish beats Boeuf Bourguignon any day — unless you are crazy about brandy!

2 pounds shank or chuck

Seasoning I
3 cloves garlic, crushed
2 whole scallions
3 slices ginger
1 tablespoon chili paste

Seasoning II
1 star anise
8 cloves
½ teaspoon Sichuan peppercorn
1 piece Chinese cinnamon (optional)
3 tablespoons dark soy sauce
1 cup water

1 tablespoon oil
1 teaspoon sugar
1 teaspoon cornstarch
1 teaspoon sesame oil

Ask the butcher to cut beef into stew pieces. Combine **Seasoning I** ingredients. Sew the first 4 items in **Seasoning II** in a cloth bag. Combine with the rest of **Seasoning II.**

In a heavy saucepan, heat 1 tablespoon oil until hot. Stir **Seasoning I** until aromatic. Add beef and stir until color changes. Add **Seasoning II.** When it boils again, cover and simmer over low heat for one hour. Stir occasionally. Add sugar and continue simmering for another half hour. Discard visible spices. *May be refrigerated or frozen and reheated.* Just before serving, thicken the sauce with cornstarch mixed with some water. Sprinkle with sesame oil and serve hot.

Tomatoes, carrots, and icicle radishes may be added in the last half hour of cooking.

糖醋排骨

Sweet and Sour Spareribs

Sweet and sour dishes are usually associated with Deep-Frying. However, this delightful dish requires only Stewing. When you have a crowd to serve, you can make a large quantity of this dish ahead of time without much effort.

> 2 pounds small pork spareribs
> 2 cloves garlic
> 3 slices ginger
> 2 whole scallions
> 1 tablespoon oil

Seasoning
> 2 tablespoons sugar
> 4 tablespoons vinegar
> 2 tablespoons dark soy sauce
> 1 tablespoon light soy sauce
> 1 tablespoon wine
> ½ cup water

> Some Stir-Fried green vegetables (optional)

Ask the butcher to cut across the bones into three strips, then separate the ribs. Crush garlic and cut scallions into 2″ sections. Heat 1 tablespoon oil in pan. Add garlic, ginger root and scallions. Stir until aromatic.

Add ribs and brown over medium heat. Transfer to a heavy pot. Add **Seasoning.** Bring to boil. Cover and simmer over low heat for 1 hour. Stir occasionally. Discard visible spices, skim fat. *May be prepared ahead up to this point, refrigerated or frozen, then reheated.*

Line bottom of serving platter with Stir-Fried Spinach or Stir-Fried Bok Choy (see p.21).

Place on ribs and serve hot.

黃燜鷄

Yellow-Smothered Chicken

You can cook this chicken even if you are too chicken to smother a live chicken! Smothering does not refer to the chicken, but to the cooking. It is a method of cooking in which the pot is never opened once the Simmering starts. The light soy sauce and chicken fat used in this recipe bring out the natural yellow color of the chicken.

1 fryer, about 3 pounds
3 cloves garlic (optional)

Marinade
3 slices ginger
2 whole scallions
1 teaspoon sugar
4 tablespoons light soy sauce
1 tablespoon wine

---

2 tablespoons chicken fat or oil
1 whole scallion, chopped

Have the butcher chop the chicken, together with skin and bones, into bite-sized pieces. Crush garlic. Smash ginger and scallions with side of the cleaver. Cut scallions into sections. Combine all **Marinade** ingredients with chicken and let stand for 15 minutes. Drain and reserve the excess.

Heat 2 tablespoons chicken fat in wok until hot. Brown garlic first and then add chicken. When chicken is also browned, transfer into a sand pot or casserole dish. Add reserved **Marinade.** Cover and simmer over low heat for 25 minutes. Try not to open the lid, but shake it occasionally to prevent sticking. Discard ginger and scallions. *May be prepared ahead and kept warm, refrigerated or frozen.* Garnish with scallions. Serve hot or cold.

Other Applications
Chicken in Oyster Sauce: Add 1 tablespoon cornstarch and 1 tablespoon oyster sauce to **Marinade.** Fresh mushrooms or soaked dried mushrooms may also be added before Simmering.

紅燜双冬

Winter Duet

Filial piety is the foremost virtue for the Chinese. Boys and girls are told stories of filial piety at a young age, one of which is about Mung Tsung, whose sick mother was hungry for bamboo shoots in the middle of winter. Where could he get any fresh vegetables in the dead of winter? Mung Tsung looked and looked, but couldn't find any. Dejected, he sat down in the bamboo forest and wept. The gods were so moved by this that they made a bamboo sprout come up through the frozen soil. An exotic variety of bamboo is called Mung Tsung Bamboo. It has spots resembling tear drops. Winter bamboo and winter mushrooms (dried mushrooms) together make an elegant banquet dish.

12 large dried mushrooms
1 18-oz. can of bamboo shoots

Seasoning
1 teaspoon sugar
1 tablespoon dark soy sauce
1 tablespoon light soy sauce
1 tablespoon wine
½ cup chicken broth

---

2 tablespoons oil
1 teaspoon cornstarch
½ teaspoon sesame oil

Soak mushrooms in cold water for 2 hours or more. Discard liquid and stems. Split each bamboo shoot lengthwise into two. Slice into thin wedges. Assemble **Seasoning.**

Heat 2 tablespoons oil in wok until hot. Add bamboo shoots and stir for 1 minute. Add mushrooms and **Seasoning**. When the liquid boils, turn heat to medium and simmer for 10 minutes. Thicken with 1 teaspoon cornstarch mixed with some water. Sprinkle with sesame oil. Serve hot or cold.

醬肉

Bean Sauce Pork

Pork is so important to the Chinese that the very character for family(家), is a pig under a roof. Chinese dwellings dating back to 2900 B.C. bear evidence of housing pigs. When the Chinese say "meat," they mean "pork." Use this dish as "wine food," meaning an appetizer, or as a snack, rolling the pork inside Thin Cakes (p.55).

    2 pounds pork*
    ½ teaspoon salt
    2 tablespoons hoisin sauce

Seasoning

    4 tablespoons dark soy sauce
    1 tablespoon wine
    1 star anise
    1 piece Chinese cinnamon
    3 slices ginger
    2 whole scallions
    ¼ cup water
    ─────────────────────────
    2 tablespoons rock candy or sugar
      fresh coriander (optional)
    1 whole scallion, shredded

*Use fresh meat with some fat, such as butt.

Rub salt and hoisin sauce *onto* meat. Let stand for 2 hours, or overnight in the refrigerator.

In a heavy pot, bring **Seasoning** to boil. Add pork. When liquid boils again, cover, turn heat low and simmer for 1 hour. Turn occasionally. Add rock candy and continue Simmering until liquid is thick and reduced in volume, but not dry, about ½ hour. Let cool. Slice against the grain into large, thin slices. Arrange on platter and pour liquid over. Garnish with scallions. Can be kept in refrigerator for several days or frozen indefinitely.

豆豉排骨

Spareribs in Black Bean Sauce

Of all the ways to cook this dish, this recipe is perhaps the least greasy and the most tasty. The **Sauce** *tastes yummy with hot, fluffy rice.*

    2 pounds small pork spareribs
    2 teaspoons salt
    1 tablespoon wine

Seasoning

    2 tablespoons fermented black beans
    3 slices ginger
    3 cloves garlic

Sauce

    1 cup water
    1 tablespoon sugar
    1 tablespoon wine
    3 tablespoons dark soy sauce
    ─────────────────────────
    1 tablespoon oil
    1 tablespoon cornstarch
    1 whole scallion, shredded
    1 fresh red chili, shredded (optional)

Ask the butcher to cut across the bones twice. Separate the ribs. Mix with salt and wine. Let stand for 20 minutes. Steam for 1 hour. Drain liquid and save for other uses.

Prepare **Seasoning** by first rinsing black beans in cold water, then mincing with the rest of the **Seasoning**. Assemble **Sauce** in a bowl.

Heat 1 tablespoon oil in wok. Stir **Seasoning** until fragrant. Add ribs and stir briefly. Add **Sauce.** Bring to boil, cover and simmer over low heat for 10 minutes. *May be prepared ahead up to this point, kept warm, refrigerated or frozen, then reheated.* Thicken with cornstarch mixed with some water. Garnish with scallion and chili shreds.

咖哩鷄飯

Chicken Curry Over Rice

My husband, George, from Southwest India, claims that Indians invented everything, but I know that the Chinese did. Of course, the world's best dishes are those dishes cooked the Chinese way. So, here is an Indian dish cooked the Chinese way. It is a meal in itself.

¹⁄₂ fryer or 1 pair chicken breasts

Marinade
- 1 teaspoon salt
- 2 teaspoons cornstarch
- 1 teaspoon wine
- 1 tablespoon light soy sauce

- 1 small onion
- 1 potato
- 2 tablespoons oil
- 2 teaspoons curry powder
- 1 cup water
  - a dash of pepper (more to taste)
- 1 recipe boiled rice (p.130)

Ask the butcher to chop the chicken into bite-sized pieces, together with the bones and skin. Toss lightly with **Marinade** and set aside for 15 minutes. Chop onion coarsely. Peel and cut potato into bite-sized cubes.

Heat 2 tablespoons oil in wok until hot. Add the following ingredients in the order listed, stirring after each addition: Onion, curry powder, chicken, potatoes and water. When the liquid boils, turn heat to medium, cover and simmer until tender, about 25 minutes. Stir occasionally. Sprinkle with pepper. *May be prepared ahead up to this point, refrigerated or frozen, then reheated.* Pour hot curry over steaming hot rice and serve.

Other Applications
Chicken Curry: Serve as a dish by itself, instead of over rice. Rice can still be served on the side.

花椒鷄丁

Sichuan Peppercorn Chicken

In the old Sichuan Province, there was a rich family whose members rarely ate together. Some night owls would return home in the wee hours of the morning and demand dinner. Tired of staying up late night after night, the chef cooked up this dish. He made large quantities of this dish and stored it in an urn, so that the latecomers could eat it hot or cold at any time.

1 fryer or 3 whole chicken breasts

Marinade
3 slices ginger
2 whole scallions
1 tablespoon soy sauce
1 teaspoon wine

Seasoning

1 teaspoon sugar
1 tablespoon wine
2 tablespoons soy sauce
¼ cup broth or water

3 dried chilies
2 tablespoons oil
1 teaspoon Sichuan peppercorn
1 teaspoon sesame oil

Skin and bone chicken. Cut into 1″ cubes. Smash scallions and ginger with side of cleaver. Cut scallions into 2″ sections. Combine with the rest of the **Marinade** and chicken. Let stand for 15 minutes. Assemble **Seasoning**. Nip off ends of chilies and shake out seeds. Cut into 1″ sections and set aside.

Heat 2 tablespoons oil in wok until very hot. Add Sichuan peppercorn. Stir briefly. Take out as many peppercorns as you can with a cooking spoon and discard. (Be careful, because some may pop up.) Fry chilies in pepper-flavored oil until black. Add chicken and stir until color changes, then add **Seasoning.** When it boils, cover and simmer over low heat for 5 minutes. Stir occasionally. Discard ginger. Sprinkle with sesame oil. Serve hot or cold.

Other Applications
For those who love to nibble on bones, don't bone the chicken.

鑲洋菇
Stuffed Mushrooms

A favorite as an appetizer or as a main dish.

24 medium-sized mushrooms,
  fresh or dried*
1 teaspoon cornstarch for dusting
2 tablespoons finely chopped ham
  or carrot

Filling
½ pound pork, ground once
4 water chestnuts, chopped
½ teaspoon salt
¼ teaspoon pepper
½ teaspoon sugar
1 teaspoon cornstarch
½ teaspoon wine
1 teaspoon light soy sauce

Sauce
½ teaspoon salt
½ teaspoon sugar
1 cup broth, seasoned w/salt

1 tablespoon cornstarch for thickening
1 teaspoon sesame oil (optional)
  coriander leaves or frozen peas

*If dried mushrooms are used, soak in warm water for 20 minutes. Drain.

Remove mushroom stems. Lay cups upside-down and dust with cornstarch. Mix **Filling** well and fill mushrooms. Sprinkle with chopped ham.

Bring **Sauce** to boil in a frying pan. Place mushrooms in it, with filled side up. Cover and simmer over medium heat for 5 minutes, basting occasionally. *May be prepared ahead up to this point, refrigerated or frozen, then re-heated.* Transfer mushrooms onto a platter, leaving **Sauce** in pan. Thicken with cornstarch mixed with some water. Sprinkle with sesame oil. Pour over mushrooms. Decorate with coriander leaves.

Other Applications
Mushroom Stuffed with Shrimp: Substitute ½ pound shrimp for pork. Clean, devein and mince. Add a few drops of ginger juice.

Vegetarian Stuffed Mushrooms: Substitute 1 cup mashed potatoes for pork; substitute a dash of salt and a dash of m.s.g. for soy sauce.

麻婆豆腐

Ma Po Bean Curd

Ma Po, the pockmarked Grandma, invented this dish in the 1860s. In her creative wok, she transformed the bland bean curd into a powerfully spicy dish. Her family food shop is still operating in Chengdu, the capital of Sichuan province. The name of the shop has been changed to "Chen's Ma Po Bean Curd Shop". Besides the famous Ma Po Bean Curd, the shop serves many other bean curd and non-bean curd dishes. It manufactures fresh bean curd daily as well. The ingredients in the following recipe are essentially the same as those used by Ma Po more than a hundred years ago.

    1 pound bean curd, preferably soft

Seasoning
    1 tablespoon fermented black beans
    3 cloves garlic
    3 slices ginger
    1 tablespoon Sichuan hot bean sauce

Sauce
    ½ teaspoon salt
    1 teaspoon sugar
    1 tablespoon soy sauce
    1 cup broth or water

    2 tablespoons oil
    ¼ pound ground beef
    1 tablespoon cornstarch
    1 teaspoon sesame oil
    ¼ teaspoon ground Sichuan pepper
    1 whole scallion, chopped

Cut bean curd into ¾ inch cubes. Rinse black beans and mince them with garlic and ginger. Assemble **Seasoning** and **Sauce** separately. Heat oil until hot. Stir **Seasoning** until fragrant. Add beef and stir until color changes. Pour **Sauce** ingredients over and let boil. Add bean curd and bring to boil again. Stir gently, cover and simmer over medium heat for 3 minutes. *May be prepared ahead up to this point, kept warm or referigerated and reheated, but not frozen.* Thicken gravy with cornstarch mixed with some water. Sprinkle with sesame oil, Sichuan pepper and scallion. Serve hot.

Other Applications
Vegetarian Ma Po Bean Curd: Omit beef.
Bean Curd in Bean Sauce: Substitute bean paste for Sichuan hot bean sauce. Omit Sichuan pepper.

茶葉蛋

Tea Eggs

During the Warring States Period (403 — 221 B.C.), there reigned quite an unreasonable king. He ordered one of his officials to produce a cock's egg in three days, or else... The official went home quite disheartened. His grandson, on finding out what was troubling his grandfather, undertook to appeal to the king. He went to the king and told him that his grandfather had found the cock's egg but could not appear in person himself because he was giving birth at home.

"Stupid boy, how can a man give birth?" roared the king. "Your Majesty, if a man can't give birth, how can a cock lay eggs?" The king appreciated the boy's wisdom and made him a high official at the age of 12. His name was Ganlo.

The following recipe is not made from cock's eggs, but hen's eggs. The dish is good for brownbagging, picnics, and long distance travel.

   1 dozen hard boiled eggs
   4 teaspoons salt
   6 tea bags
   2 tablespoons dark soy sauce
   4 star anise

② Gently crack eggs against each other. Don't peel. Place in a pot and cover with water. Add the rest of the ingredients. Bring to boil. Turn heat low, cover and simmer for two hours. Let cool in the liquid. May be kept in the liquid at room temperature for a few days. If the eggs become too salty, dilute the liquid to taste with water.

①

②

砂鍋獅子頭

Lion's Head Casserole

Lion's Head is a dish for New Year's Day. When used on that day, there must be four meatballs, not only to symbolize the four seasons, but also to signify the four blessings of 福祿壽康 *(Happiness, Prosperity, Longevity, and Health). and Health).*

1 head Chinese cabbage, 2 to 3 pounds

Meat Mixture
2 slices ginger, finely chopped
2 scallion stems, chopped
6 water chestnuts, chopped
1 pound ground pork*
1 teaspoon sugar
1 tablespoon cornstarch
2 tablespoons soy sauce

½ cup oil
2 tablespoons cornstarch
2 tablespoons water
2 cups broth, seasoned with salt

*Ask the butcher to grind the pork only once. The meat should not be too lean. If too lean, add ½ cup bean curd or a slice of stale bread, first soaked in water and then squeezed dry.

Wash cabbage. Cut across into 2″ sections. Blanch in boiling water for 1 minute. Drain. Line bottom of casserole dish with ¾ cabbage. Reserve the rest.

In a large bowl, stir **Meat Mixture** in one direction until it develops elasticity, about 4 minutes. *Can also be done in a food processor (see p.14).* Shape into 4 balls.

Heat oil in wok until hot. Mix cornstarch with water to make a paste. ② Coat one meatball in it and lower gently into oil. Turn and brown all surfaces. (It will take less than 1 minute.) Carefully lay it in the cabbage-lined casserole. Repeat with the other three balls. Add broth. Cover with reserved cabbage. Bring to boil. Turn heat low, cover and simmer for 1 hour. *May be kept warm, refrigerated or frozen.* Serve hot.

①

②

BOILING METHOD

Boiling, 煮 ,is cooking food in rapidly boiling water and continuing to apply high heat until the food is cooked. It may take only a few minutes, e.g., *Wonton* and *Jiaotze*;or it may require ½ hour or longer, e.g., Laba Porridge.

Wonton, Jiaotze and Laba Porridge are all made using a single cooking method, namely, *Boiling.* The same method is also used in combination with other methods, such as Boiling and Cold-Mixing used in Cold-Mixed String Beans.

Boiling may sound simple. And many dishes in this category are indeed quite simple to make. However, very elaborate dishes are also made using a version of the Boiling method. Ingredients are often cooked first; the flavors are blended by final boiling of the various items assembled in the pot; and the broth is thickened by adding cornstarch paste. This is called *Assembling,* 燴 . Often the ingredients are expensive and hard to find, and the dishes are used

魚翅湯

Shark's Fin Soup

Makes 10 cups

Shark's Fin Soup is a banquet dish, and an expensive one. The price of a Chinese banquet depends on the number of dishes and the scarcity of the ingredients. The Chinese believe the rarer the ingredient the better. While shark's fin and dried scallops appear at rather expensive banquets, bear's paws (if you can afford them) are reserved to honor your most respected guest. Personally, I prefer to leave my precious pawed friends free to roam the wilderness.

1 whole chicken breast

Marinade
1 teaspoon salt
1 teaspoon cornstarch
1 teaspoon wine

6 dried mushrooms
½ bamboo shoot
½ cup snow peas, stringed
4 cups broth, seasoned with salt
3 slices ginger
2 whole scallions
2 10-oz. cans shark's fins

3 tablespoons cornstarch
3 egg whites, beaten
¼ teaspoon white pepper
1 tablespoon cooked shredded Smithfield ham

Skin and bone chicken breast. Shred and combine with **Marinade**. Let stand for 15 minutes. Soak mushrooms in warm water for 15 minutes. Discard water and stems. Shred mushrooms, bamboo shoot and snow peas. Bring broth to boil. Add ginger, scallions, mushrooms and bamboo shoot. Boil for 2 minutes. Add chicken. Stir to separate. When it boils, add shark's fin, liquid and all. Bring to boil again, add snow peas. Discard ginger and scallions. Thicken with cornstarch mixed with some water. Slowly pour in egg whites, while stirring with the other hand. Pour into tureen. Garnish with pepper and ham. Serve hot.

臘八粥

Laba Porridge

Makes 12 cups

Laba Porridge is also called "Buddha's Porridge," and is traditionally eaten on the 8th day (ba) of the 12th lunar month (la), the day of Buddha's Enlightenment. Because Buddhism forbids all forms of killing, many Buddhists are vegetarians. In the old days, a few days before the festival, the monks would go out and beg for grain to make Laba Porridge. This was offered to the Buddha, and then distributed to the poor. It is believed that whoever eats the porridge will be blessed. On a cold winter day, if this hearty, sweet porridge does not nourish your soul, it will at least warm your body.

12 red jujubes
2 tablespoons dried red beans
2 tablespoons dried mung beans
¼ cup lotus seeds
1 cup glutinous rice
2 tablespoons barley
12 cups water
2 tablespoons dried dragon's eyes or black raisins
    brown sugar to taste
4 tablespoons roasted nuts, any kind

Soak jujubes, red and mung beans in cold water for 6 hours. Drain. De-seed jujubes. Rinse lotus seeds, rice and barley. Place the first 6 ingredients in large pot with 12 cups water. Bring to boil, turn heat to medium, partially cover and boil for 30 minutes. Add dragon's eyes and brown sugar and cook for 5 minutes more. *May be prepared ahead and re-heated.* Before serving, garnish with nuts and serve hot.

餛 飩 湯
Wonton Soup

Makes 60 *Wontons*
Unlike the Stir-Fried recipes which cannot be doubled, you can make tons of Wontons *and keep them in freezer boxes between layers of wax paper, if the meat has not been previously frozen. When you feel like having* Wontons, *just drop a few directly into boiling water and cook for 5-6 minutes.*

Filling
- ½ pound pork, ground once
- 1 teaspoon sugar
- a pinch of pepper
- a pinch of m.s.g. (optional)
- 2 teaspoons cornstarch
- 2 tablespoons water
- 1 tablespoon soy sauce
- 2 teaspoons wine
- 1 teaspoon sesame oil
- ¼ cup water chestnuts, chopped

- 1 pound thin *Wonton* wrappers, about 60
- 8 cups broth, seasoned with salt
- 2 teaspoons light soy sauce
- 1 cup spinach or bok choy
- 1 whole scallion, chopped

Combine **Filling** ingredients in a small bowl. With a pair of chopsticks, stir them in a circular motion until all liquid is absorbed. Wrap *Wonton* skins in damp cloth, unwrap only a few at a time before using. ② Make *Wontons* by placing ½ teaspoon of **Filling** in each piece of skin. ③ Moisten edges with water; fold skin in half and pinch edges to seal securely; ④ Moisten one side with water; ⑤ Bring to the other side and press together. Remember not to over-fill; ⑥ and pinch them securely. *May be wrapped ahead of time, refrigerated or frozen between waxed paper.*

Bring a large pot of water to boil over high heat. In the meantime, heat the broth over medium heat. Drop all the *Wontons* into the boiling water, a few at a time. Boil over high heat for 3 to 4 minutes if fresh, 5 to 6 minutes if frozen. Drain immediately and transfer into a tureen. By this time the broth should also be boiling. Add soy sauce, spinach or bok choy. When the soup boils again, pour it over the *Wontons*. Garnish with scallion and serve.

Other Applications:
Fried Wontons: Fry wrapped *Wontons*, a few at a time, in 350°F oil until golden brown, about 1 minute on each side. Serve with Sweet and Sour Pineapple Dip (p.130) or Lemon Dip (p.130).

酒釀元宵

Rice Dumplings and Wine Rice Soup

Yuan-Hsiao, *Rice Dumplings*, are a festive food, eaten at the winter solstice, the shortest day of the year, as well as on the 15th day of the first lunar month which marks the end of the New Year season. This recipe calls for miniature Yuan-Hsiao. *The slightly alcoholic wine rice gives this sweet dish a refreshing zing. Serve it as a snack, a dessert, or a banquet course.*

    1 cup glutinous rice flour
    5 tablespoons warm water
    4 cups water
    2 cups wine rice*
    1 egg, beaten
      sugar to taste

*Wine rice can be either purchased in jars from an Oriental grocer or made at home (p.132).

Mix rice flour with 5 tablespoons warm water to form a firm dough. ② Shape it into pencil-sized sticks by rolling between palms. ③ Break the sticks into small pieces.

Bring 4 cups of water to boil. Drop dices into water. Boil until pieces surface, about a minute. Add wine rice. When the liquid boils again, turn heat low, add egg and stir gently. Sweeten with sugar if necessary. Serve hot. May be prepared ahead of time and re-heated.

Other Applications
Yuan-Hsiao and Orange Soup: Substitute wine rice with 3 oranges. Cut across the grain as you would with grapefruit. Scoop out pulp with a spoon and squeeze out the juice. Put both in soup. Omit the egg.

①

②

③

糯米糍

Glutinous Rice Balls

Makes 16 balls
Instead of the traditional hard pounding in a mortar to prepare the glutinous rice for wrapping, I have developed a much easier way However, the new Glutinous Rice Balls tend to harden the next day. So make them the day you plan to serve them.

Dough
    2 cups glutinous rice flour
    ¼ cup cornstarch
    2 tablespoons sugar
    1 tablespoon lard or margarine
    ¾ cup water
    ―――――――――――――――――
    ½ cup dousha (p.140)
    2 cups sweetened coconut flakes
    8 red maraschino cherries

Combine the **Dough** ingredients and knead into a firm dough. Divide the dousha into 16 portions and shape them into balls. Divide the **Dough** into 16 portions also. Shape each portion into a cup. Put a dousha ball in each cup. ② Close the top by gently gathering the **Dough**. ③ Shape into a round ball.

Bring a large pot of water to boil over high heat. Drop the filled rice balls into the water. Stir gently to prevent them from sticking to the bottom. Boil in rapidly-boiling water for 8 minutes. Lift the balls up with a slotted spoon and set them on a plate.

Put coconut flakes on another plate. Roll the balls on the flakes until coated. ④ Decorate each with half a cherry. Serve them at room temperature. Do not refrigerate.

Other Applications:
Sesame Seed Balls: Substitute ½ cup white sesame seeds for coconut flakes. Toast seeds in 250°F oven for 15 minutes. Cool before using.

①

③

②

④

餃 子

Jiaotze

Make 48 *Jiaotze*

Jiaotze are a great cook-in! When I entertain with Jiaotze, I invite everyone into the kitchen, as in Northern China, where Jiaotze-making is a family affair, one person rolling the dough, and the others wrapping it around the **Filling** — *which can be meat, vegetables, or a mixture. Its ingot-shape made it a symbol of wealth in the old days when money was ingot-shaped; therefore, it is a must for New Year celebrations in Northern China.*

Filling
1 cup chopped cabbage
1 teaspoon salt
1 pound ground beef or pork*
¼ teaspoon pepper
2 tablespoons soy sauce
1 teaspoon sesame oil
2 scallion stems, finely chopped

Dip
light soy sauce
vinegar
chili oil
sesame oil
minced garlic

1 pound *Jiaotze* skins **

*Add 2 tablespoons oil if the meat is too lean

**Buy from an Oriental grocer or make it at home: Use 3 cups flour and ¾ cup cold water. Follow the same instructions as for *Guotieh* wrappers (p.56). Divide the dough into 48 instead of 36 portions.

Mix cabbage with 1 teaspoon salt. Knead as if kneading dough. Squeeze out the juice and discard. Mix with the rest of **Filling** ingredients. Wrap *Jiaotze* skins in damp cloth, unwrap only a few at a time before making *Jiaotze*. Moisten edges with water if necessary. Follow *Guotieh* wrapping instructions to wrap *Jiaotze* (p. 56, steps 2 to 4).

When ready to cook, bring a large pot of water to boil. Drop all the *Jiaotze* into the water, a few at a time. Boil over high heat for 3 to 4 minutes if fresh; 5 to 6 minutes if frozen. Add a bit of cold water whenever the pot is about to boil over. Drain immediately and spread over a platter. Serve with **Dip** set in separate bowls and let each person help himself (herself) to it.

PLUNGING METHOD 汆

Plunging, 汆 , is a quick way to whip up marvelous soups. The soup base is brought to a boil first, then small pieces of food are dropped in. The cooking is very brief, often completed even before the soup comes to a second boil. Morsels in the soup are very tender because they don't have a chance to get tough by overcooking.

When Plunging is a do-it-yourself operation, as in fire pot cooking, it is called *Rinsing,* 涮 , (see Chrysanthemum Fire Pot). In other types of soup, the solids and liquid are eaten together; but in the fire pot, you first eat the solids, served with an assortment of condiments spread on the table. The broth is savored afterwards.

6. PLUNGING DEMONSTRATION RECIPES

蛋花湯

Egg Drop Soup

Makes 4 cups

My students nicknamed this soup "Stone Soup," referring to the children's story of how a soldier talked an old lady into making a pot of soup when she had "nothing" on hand. The soldier replied: "Why don't you use a stone?" The old lady polished a stone and put it in the pot. The hungry soldier asked: "Do you have some potatoes?" She had; and she put them in. Other items were added one after another, until a hearty soup was steaming hot. Incidentally, the effort you have to put in for this recipe, like the materials the old lady said she had, is also "nothing."

    4 cups broth, seasoned with salt

Seasoning
    1 teaspoon light soy sauce
    a few drops of vinegar
    a pinch of pepper

---

    1 egg, slightly beaten
    1 whole scallion, chopped

Bring broth to boil. Add **Seasoning.** Add egg and stir gently. Turn off heat and sprinkle with scallion. Serve hot.

Other Applications

Egg Drop and Spinach Soup: After adding **Seasoning,** add a cup of spinach, washed and broken into 3" pieces. When the liquid boils again, add egg.

Egg Drop and Laver Soup: Crush 1 sheet of laver and place in soup tureen, pour Egg Drop Soup over.

Three-Color Soup

Makes 8 cups

The colors are limited only by your imagination! See colorful alternatives suggested below to exercise your culinary skills:

    ¼ pound spinach
    ½ pound bean curd
    1 tomato
    6 cups broth, any kind,
        seasoned with salt

Seasoning
    1 tablespoon light soy sauce
    a pinch of pepper
    a few drops of vinegar

Soak spinach in large quantity of water to get rid of sand. Separate leaves from roots. Scrape roots and split the larger ones. Cut bean curd into 1" x 1" x ½" pieces. Peel tomato and cut into wedges.

Bring 6 cups of broth to boil. Add the items in the following order, bring to boil after each addition: **Seasoning,** bean curd, tomato, spinach stems and spinach leaves.

Other Applications:

Use your imagination to make other colorful soups. For instance, substitute snow peas for spinach; bamboo shoots for bean curd; ham for tomato. Also add other items such as dried mushrooms (pre-soaked) and eggs (beaten). Always add items that take the longest to cook first. Throw in many colorful things like the painter splashing colors on the canvas. Have fun!

榨菜肉片湯
Jahtsai and Meat Slice Soup

Makes 8 cups
The secret of the tender meat, even without any cornstarch, is that cold water is used to start the cooking process. This spicy and appetizing soup is one of my favorites.

- 6 dried mushrooms
- 2 oz. bean threads
- ½ pound pork
- 1 piece *jahtsai*
- 6 cups cold water
- 1 tablespoon light soy sauce
- 1 tablespoon wine
- salt to taste
- 1 whole scallion, chopped

Soak dried mushrooms in warm water for 20 minutes. Discard water and stems. ② Quarter. Soak bean threads in warm water for 5 minutes. Discard liquid. ③ Cut across twice. Slice pork into thin slices. Rinse *jahtsai* (unless you like the soup very spicy) and slice thin into ½ cup.

Put mushrooms, pork and *jahtsai* in 6 cups of cold water in a pot. Bring to boil over medium flame. Remove residue. Add bean threads, soy sauce and wine. Add salt to taste. Bring to boil again. *May be prepared ahead up to this point. Keep warm or refrigerate and reheat.* Garnish with scallion and serve hot.

西洋菜鷄片湯
Chicken Slices and Watercress Soup (Top Picture)

Makes 8 cups
While the Westerners associate watercress with Chinese food, the Chinese call the vegetable "hsi yang tsai," Western Vegetables!

- 1 whole chicken breast

Marinade
- ¼ teaspoon salt
- 1 teaspoon cornstarch
- 1 teaspoon wine

- 6 dried mushrooms
- 1 bunch watercress
- ⅛ teaspoon ground white pepper
- ½ teaspoon sesame oil (optional)
- 6 cups chicken broth, seasoned with salt

Bone chicken breast. Discard skin, bones and tendons. Cut into ⅛" slices. Combine with **Marinade** and set aside.

Soak dried mushrooms in warm water for 20 minutes. Discard water and stems. Slice thin. Wash watercress. Put pepper and sesame oil in tureen.

Bring broth to boil. Add mushrooms and boil for 2 minutes. Add chicken. Stir to separate. When it boils again, add watercress, pour into tureen immediately and serve.

Other Applications:
Chicken Slices and Cucumber Soup: Substitute one tender cucumber for watercress. Peel, split it lengthwise, and slice. Add cucumber and mushrooms at the same time.

芙蓉鷄片湯

Chicken Fuyung Soup

Makes 5 cups
Fuyung, *hibiscus, is much loved by Chinese poets and artists. Bai Jyuyee (772-846 A.D.), the famous poet of the Tang Dynasty, often compared beautiful faces to Fuyung. This soup, made of egg white and white chicken meat, resembles the beautiful flower.*

   1 whole chicken breast

Marinade
   ¼ teaspoon salt
   1 teaspoon cornstarch
   1 teaspoon wine

      a pinch of ground white pepper
   ½ teaspoon sesame oil (optional)
   2 egg whites
   2 tablespoons water
   4 cups chicken broth, seasoned with salt
   2 tablespoons cornstarch (for thickening)
   1 stalk fresh coriander or
      whole scallion, chopped

Skin and bone chicken breast. Slice thin. ② Combine with **Marinade**. Place pepper and sesame oil in tureen. Beat egg whites in 2 tablespoons water.

Bring broth to boil. Thicken with cornstarch mixed with some water. Add chicken, stir to separate. As soon as the broth boils again, turn heat low, pour in egg white slowly with one hand and stir with the other. Pour into tureen. Sprinkle with coriander. Additional items such as shredded bamboo shoots can be added before soup is thickened.

Other Applications
Shrimp Fuyung Soup: Substitute ½ pound shrimp, cleaned, deveined and rinsed, for chicken.

Crab Fuyung Soup: Substitute 6 oz. crabmeat, either fresh or canned, for chicken. Do not marinate.

Fish Fuyung Soup: Substitute ½ pound fish fillet for chicken. Cut into ⅓" slices.

西湖牛肉羹

West Lake Beef Soup

Makes 6 cups
Water is not served at the Chinese dinner table but soup is. You need to serve a lot of soups, plain and fancy. This one looks and tastes fancy, but is easy to make.

½ pound sirloin or flank

Marinade
1 teaspoon cornstarch
1 teaspoon sugar
1 teaspoon wine
1 tablespoon soy sauce

4 cups broth, seasoned with salt
2 tablespoons cornstarch
2 egg whites, beaten
⅛ teaspoon pepper
1 whole scallion, shredded

Slice beef against grain. Combine with **Marinade** and let stand for 15 minutes.

Bring broth to boil. Add beef and stir. When the broth boils again, thicken with cornstarch mixed with some water. Slowly pour in egg white while stirring. Pour into tureen. Garnish with pepper and scallion.

蟹肉玉米羹
Velvet Corn and Crab Soup

Makes 6 cups
Ever since canned corn was imported into China, velvet corn soups have sprouted up like spring bamboo shoots after rain. This particular soup is very popular among both Americans and the Chinese. It is so simple to make!

    3 cups chicken broth, seasoned w/salt
    1 17-oz. can creamed corn
    3 tablespoons cornstarch
    4 to 6 oz. crab meat, fresh or canned
    1 egg white, beaten
    1 teaspoon Smithfield ham, finely
        chopped (optional)
        a pinch of ground white pepper

Bring broth and corn to boil. Thicken with cornstarch mixed with some water. Add crab meat and stir. As soon as soup comes to boil again, turn heat low. ② Pour in the egg white slowly with one hand and stir with the other. Pour soup into a tureen, garnish with pepper and ham. Serve hot.

Other Applications:
Velvet Corn and Chicken Soup: Substitute 1 cup chicken breast meat for crab meat. Set blender on low speed and blend chicken until smooth. Mix with a pinch of salt and ½ tablespoon cornstarch.

Corn and Egg Drop Soup: Omit crab meat. Use a whole egg instead of just the white.

酸辣湯
Sour Hot Soup

Makes 8 cups
This northern dish is exactly what it says: Sour and Hot. When the northern wind blows, one is warmed and comforted by a bowl of this thick, hot soup. Be creative, find whatever leftovers you can in your refrigerator and put them in the soup — meat, chicken, shrimp, crabmeat, vegetables — of course, you can make it from scratch as follows:

    1 tablespoon wood ears
    ½ pound bean curd
    1 small bamboo shoot
    1 medium-size tomato
    ½ pound pork or beef
    1 teaspoon cornstarch
    1 teaspoon wine

Seasoning
    ½ teaspoon pepper
    ½ teaspoon sugar
    1 tablespoon dark soy sauce
    1 tablespoon vinegar
    ½ teaspoon sesame oil
    1 whole scallion, chopped

    4 cups broth, seasoned w/salt
    3 tablespoons cornstarch
    1 egg, beaten

Soak wood ears in warm water for 10 minutes. Drain and shred if large ones are used. Shred bean curd, bamboo shoot and tomato. Shred meat, mix with cornstarch and wine. Place **Seasoning** in soup tureen.

Bring broth to boil. Add vegetables and meat in the order listed above, stir and bring to boil again after each addition. *May be prepared up to this point, kept warm; or refrigerated and reheated.* Thicken with cornstarch mixed with some water. Add egg and stir gently. Pour soup into the tureen and serve hot.

Other Applications:
Use chicken or shrimp in place of or in addition to the meat.

火鍋

Chrysanthemum Fire Pot

Serves 10
Chinese have been eating chrysanthemums for centuries. Only the large white ones are used for food. The large, colored ones are believed to be poisonous, while the small, daisy-like chrysanthemums of different colors are dried to make tea. This is a one-dish meal for the one who complains about last-minute cooking. Prepare everything ahead of time, and let your guests do the cooking themselves. Plan to enjoy a relaxed meal around the fire pot into which each person leisurely puts his or her favorite morsels. Set a rice bowl, a pair of chopsticks and a china spoon for each person.

    2 to 4 quarts broth
    8 dried mushrooms
    2 carrots
    1 pound Chinese cabbage
    1 bunch white chrysanthemums
    1 pound bean curd
    2 2-oz. bundles bean threads
    1 pound lean pork
    1 pound shrimp
    1 pound fish fillet
    2 whole chicken breasts
    1 pound lean beef
    ½ pound spinach

Condiments

    2 tablespoons sesame paste
      light soy sauce
      vinegar
      satay sauce
      sesame oil
      chopped scallions
   10 eggs (in shells)

Fill the fire pot* ⅔ full with broth. Light charcoal outdoors 30 minutes before dinner. The above items are listed in order of cooking time required, with the first one taking the longest time. Prepare them as follows:

Soak dried mushrooms in warm water for 15 minutes. Discard water and stems. Quarter. Peel carrots and shred. Wash Chinese cabbage and cut across into 1½″ sections. Wash chrysanthemums. Cut bean curd into 1″ x 1″ x ½″ pieces. Soak bean threads in warm water for 5 minutes. Drain and cut through threads twice.

Slice pork and beef into thin, large slices. (Meat slices easier if partially frozen.) Shell, devein, and rinse shrimp. Split each into two pieces if large. Cut fish into 1″ × 2″ × ⅓″ slices. Skin and bone chicken, cut into thin, large slices. Rinse spinach thoroughly. Cut large leaves in two. Arrange items attractively on platters.

Add 6 tablespoons water to sesame paste, a little at a time, stir while adding, until a thin, smooth paste is formed. Set in a small bowl. Put the other **Condiments** in individual bowls also.

Seat the guests. Instruct them to assemble **Condiments** in their individual rice bowls. Invite guests to drop food pieces into the boiling broth, then take them out and dip them into their own bowl of **Condiments** before eating. If you like egg yolk, beat it in with the **Condiments**. Drop the egg white into the broth. It will solidify quickly.

The liquid may be consumed at any time, but usually is saved for last. Add more broth as needed. When the dinner is about over, set a small bowl of water over the chimney of the pot to smother the fire.

Serve Steamed Buns, Silver Thread Rolls, or rice with the Fire Pot.

* If you don't have a fire pot, use an electric wok or pan.

Other Applications:

Ten-Scenery Fire Pot: In place of the raw meats, choose several from the following: Red-Cooked Pork, Puffed Shrimp Balls, Fish Balls (buy from an Oriental Grocer), and sliced Smithfield ham. Boil celery cabbage down in broth first, then arrange everything on top. Cook briefly before bringing to the table. If you don't cook at the table you do not need to light a charcoal fire or buy a fire pot.

②

STEAMING METHOD 蒸

Chinese *Steaming*,蒸 , is different from Western methods of steaming vegetables over a perforated expandable metal steamer or standing broccoli stems in a little bit of boiling water in a covered pot. In Chinese Steaming, only the steam comes into contact with the food, not the boiling water.

The Chinese steamer is the counterpart of the American oven, and just as versatile. Dainty pastries, *Dim Sum,* are steamed in steamers. Most cake recipes which call for baking can be steamed. They will come out moist, and not crusty. A whole fish, chicken, duck, or ham can also be steamed. Cut-up or ground meat is steamed and molded into an attractive shape. Steaming is also used in combination with other methods such as Smoking (Smoked Fish), or Stewing (Spareribs in Black Bean Sauce).

Most steamed recipes can be cooked in the oven or microwave oven in a covered casserole dish. Microwaving produces a taste closest to steaming, particularly for fish. Rub one tablespoon oil over fish to prevent drying.

You can cook, reheat, and keep food warm in a steamer. You can also cook at the last minute, without the last-minute hassle. Two or three or more dishes can be prepared in advance and set in the steamer together with the rice, so let the steamer do the last-minute work itself, while you chat with your guests or do your last-minute Stir-Frying.

Read the following instructions, and the description of steamers (p. 135) before you steam:

When Using A Metal Steamer
Separate the tiers from the pot. Fill the pot with two inches of water. (More if steaming time is longer than 30 minutes.) ① Cover and bring water to rolling boil. ② While waiting for the water to boil, set the food to be steamed in a heat-proof dish and place it on the tier. *Dim Sum* can be placed directly on the tiers lined with a damp cloth. ③ When the water boils, turn off the heat, open the cover, and fan to cool the air, so that the steam won't burn your hands. Steam is very hot! ④ Set the tiers on the pot, cover and return the heat to high, unless otherwise specified. Have a kettle of boiling water ready on another burner and add it when the level gets low.

When Using A Bamboo Steamer
Follow the same instructions as for the metal steamer. ⑤ Because the bamboo steamer is not equipped with a pot, you need to set the steamer in a wok or a pot which is larger than the steamer. Because extensive boiling destroys the wok seasoning, you may have to re-season the wok after steaming.

When Using A Make-Shift Steamer
⑥ Place an empty can, with both ends opened, in a large pot. Add water to the level that is at least 1" lower than the top of the can. This is to prevent the boiling water from reaching the food. ⑦ Set the food to be steamed in a heat-proof dish and place it on the can. Cover and steam the same way as above. Check the water level often. When steaming a long fish, set on two cans in an oval roasting pan.

竹節牛盅

Beef in Bamboo Bowls

Makes 12 servings

This extraordinary banquet dish requires only ordinary skills. You need twelve little soup bowls and a steamer. Traditionally, this dish is cooked in little bamboo cups and transferred to soup bowls. Since bamboo cups are hard to find in the States, use little bowls instead.

Meat Mixture
1 pound sirloin
3 dried scallops*
1 cup warm water
1 tablespoon wine
6 dried mushrooms
1 cup water chestnuts
2 tablespoons soy sauce
½ teaspoon salt
⅛ teaspoon ground pepper

4 cups broth, seasoned with salt
1 stalk fresh coriander

*Substitute 3 tablespoons dried shrimp for dried scallops. Soak for just 10 minutes.

Have the butcher grind the beef twice. (You may grind the meat at home in a food processor, see p. 14.) Soak dried scallops in 1 cup of warm water and 1 tablespoon wine overnight. Drain and reserve liquid. Chop scallops finely.

Soak mushrooms in warm water for 20 minutes. Discard liquid and stems. Chop. Chop water chestnuts coarsely. Mix **Meat Mixture** thoroughly. Gradually pour in broth and reserved liquid, stirring as you go. Place food in 12 bamboo cups or small bowls, about ¾ full.

Bring water in steamer to boil. Set bowls on steamer rack. Cover the steamer, and steam over high flame for 15 minutes. *May be kept warm in the steamer briefly. Prolonged stay in the warm steamer tends to toughen the meat.* Garnish each bowl with a sprig of coriander and serve hot.

湖南蒸魚

Hunan Steamed Fish

"Gentlemen do not eat overturned fish." There is a double meaning to "overturned fish" — either a reincarnated fish or a fish turned over to the other side after one side is consumed. This old saying must have been created by some smart servant. If gentlemen eat both sides of the fish, there will be none left for the servants who eat leftovers. Few of us have servants nowadays. Therefore, you may eat both sides of the fish and still remain a gentleman or a lady.

This dish is as exciting as it is easy to make. The most important skill required is the ability to pick a strictly fresh fish, one with bulging eyes, red gills, shining scales, and firm meat. Increase the number of chilies if you love hot food as the Hunanese do.

    1 fish* (1 to 1½ pounds)
    1 teaspoon salt
Seasoning
2 tablespoons fermented black beans
1 thick slice ginger
1 whole scallion
3 fresh red chilies
1 tablespoon light soy sauce
1 tablespoon wine

1 tablespoon sesame oil

2 tablespoons oil (optional)

*Use any fresh water or sea fish, with mild flavor and light meat, such as rock fish, flounder, bass, or shad. Use one section of the shad, leave the scales on, split open.

Have the fish salesperson scale and clean the fish, but leave the head and tail on. As soon as you bring the fish home from the market, make slashes across the body, 1½" apart. Rub the fish with salt inside and out. Leave it in the refrigerator until ready to use.

Prepare **Seasoning** as follows: Rinse black beans in cold water. Shred ginger as fine as possible to fill 1 tablespoon. Shred scallions. Cut across chilies to make rings and discard seeds, unless you want the dish very spicy. Combine all **Seasoning** ingredients. Pour over fish.

Bring water in steamer to boil. Set fish in a heat-proof platter. Steam for 10 to 12 minutes. Remove from steamer.

Heat 2 tablespoons oil until very hot. Sprinkle over fish and serve hot.

Other Applications:
Microwaved Whole Fish: Instead of Steaming, cover and microwave for 8 to 10 minutes, rotate once.

扣蝦餅

Shrimp Custard

My father tells us how bean threads were made in a little village in his home province of Hunan: A thick fluid, made of mung beans and water, was poured into a large sieve from the second floor. By the time the fluid dripped to ground level, a thin, even thread was formed. Someone caught the threads and hung them on clothes lines to dry. Today bean threads are made like most other things: in a factory!

  1 pound raw shrimp

Marinade
  ½ teaspoon salt
  ¼ teaspoon ginger root juice*
  ½ teaspoon sesame oil
  1 teaspoon wine

  2 oz. bean threads
  4 water chestnuts, chopped
  3 eggs
  ½ teaspoon salt
  1 cup chicken broth
    sesame oil for greasing
    fresh coriander for decoration

*Squeeze ginger juice with garlic press

Shell and devein shrimp. Rinse in water and drain. Combine with **Marinade**. Let stand for 10 minutes. Soak bean threads in warm water for 10 minutes. Drain. Cut through the threads several times. Mix with water chestnuts. Grease a shallow bowl with sesame oil. Line the bottom of bowl with shrimp. ① Cover with thread mixture. Pour the mixture of eggs, salt and broth over.

Bring water in steamer to boil. Set the bowl in steamer. Cover and steam over medium heat until the eggs are set, about 30 minutes. Remove from steamer. ② Cover with a serving platter. Invert onto the platter. Decorate with coriander and serve hot.

①

②

饅頭
Mantow (Steamed Buns)

Makes 12 buns

Juger Liang, 諸葛亮 *, considered one of the wisest men who ever lived, was the prime minister of the Kingdom of Shu (now Sichuan Province) during 221-234 A.D. He conquered a barbarian tribe ruled by Meng Huoh,* 孟獲 *, seven different times. The last time, Meng Huoh bowed to the superior wisdom and strategy of his conqueror, forswearing any further fights. The war having been settled honorably for both sides, Meng Huoh accompanied Juger Liang to his Kingdom of Shu. En route, they had to cross a river where, according to the barbarous tradition, a human head had to be sacrificed to ensure safe crossing. The wise Juger Liang suggested that if an innocent man were sacrificed, his ghost would demand satisfaction, requiring further sacrifices; so why not sacrifice something which looks like a human head? He ordered a huge bun, shaped like a head, to be dumped into the river. They crossed the river safely. Subsequently, steamed buns were made, the feature of a human head giving way to a simple bun. The name of the dish is* Mantou, 饅頭 *, phonetically the same as "Barbarian's Head," but one of the two characters is written differently, including the radical for food.*

Mantou *is used in North China as rice is used in the South. Either serve it in place of bread at a Chinese meal; or, stuff red-cooked meat or smoked meat in it to make sandwiches.*

  1 recipe Yeast Dough (p.132)
 12 pieces of waxed paper,
     1½ inches square

Roll dough into a long sausage. ② Cut it into 12 or more equal portions. ③ Sprinkle with flour. ④ Roll each into a round ball. ⑤ Set the balls on waxed paper, apart from each other. Cover with cloth. Let rise again for 30 minutes.

Bring water in steamer to boil. Set buns on the steamer rack, apart from each other. Steam over high heat for 12 minutes. Allow steam to subside for a few seconds before uncovering the steamer. May be refrigerated or frozen. Re-heat in steamer or microwave oven.

銀絲捲
Silver Thread Rolls

Makes 24 rolls

A banquet is no place for the ordinary; and to the Chinese everyday rice is too ordinary to be served at an extraordinary banquet. Instead, fancy Dim Sum *dishes are served to tickle one's palate. They can be sweet or savory, or alternate between the two. Here is a not-too-sweet sweet banquet dish from Hunan which can also be used as a snack.*

  1 recipe Yeast Dough (p.132)
  6 tablespoons lard or shortening
 ½ cup sugar
  2 tablespoons minced candied fruit
 24 pieces of waxed paper,
     1½ inches square

Roll half of the dough into a 12-inch square. ② Smear lard and sugar over. ③ Roll up into a cylinder. ④ Flatten slightly and cut into ¼" strips. Divide the strips into 12 bundles. Stretch each bundle slightly. ⑤ Wind it around the index finger. Place the end on top of the coiled bun. ⑥ Sprinkle top with minced fruit. Place on waxed paper. Set rolls on counter, separating them from each other. Cover with cloth and let rise for 30 minutes. Repeat with the other half.

Bring water in steamer to boil. Arrange rolls on steamer tiers, apart from each other. Steam over high heat for 8 minutes. Allow steam to subside for a few seconds before uncovering the steamer. May be refrigerated or frozen. Re-heat in steamer or microwave oven.

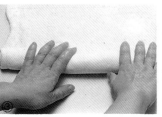

BAKING METHOD 烤

Home ovens are rarely found in China. *Roasting,* 烤 , is done in restaurants and specialty food shops. Chinese roasting is different from Western roasting. Marinated meat is hooked onto a rack and hung in an oven. During the course of the roasting, the food is basted and rotated manually. Although Chinese cook differently, roasting can be adapted to American ovens.

To make Chinese Barbecued Pork in an American oven, marinated pork strips are hung on paper clips and roasted in the oven. Ideally, Peking Duck should also be hung in similar fashion. Unfortunately, most home ovens are not tall enough to hang a duck in them. Therefore, we have to place the duck in a pan, and turn it during the course of the roasting.

Baking bread and pastries is a different process, primarily because the ovens are heated differently. In the old-fashioned *Shaobing* (Roasted Bun) shops the bread was stuck to the oven wall to bake. The oven was made of clay, not of metal. However, today's *Shaobing* ovens are similar to the ovens found all over the world.

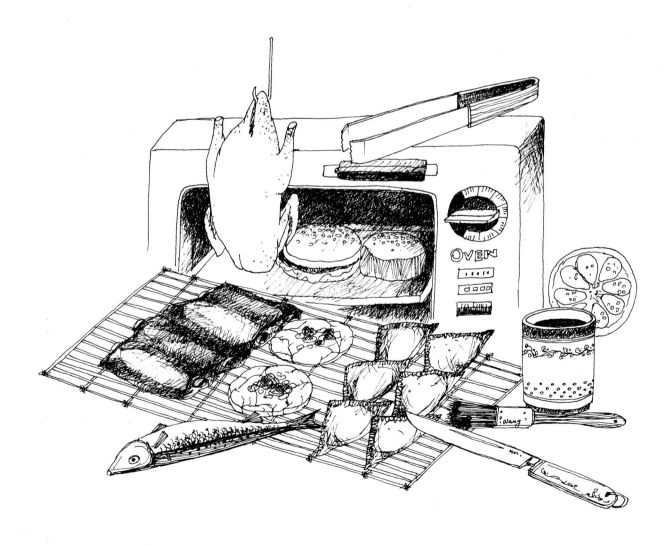

北京烤鸭

Peking Duck

Traditional Peking Duck is prepared in a complicated manner. Air is first blown into the duck between the skin and the meat. It is next dried in the air, then roasted in the oven , while being brushed with syrup. The air-drying and roasting are repeated once. The total roasting takes less than an hour.

Most ducks come from our supermarkets frozen. The skin is already broken, so blowing in air is next to impossible. Besides this, western ovens heat differently, and are not generally tall enough to accomodate a duck. Nevertheless, the following recipe is simple and close to authentic Peking Duck prepared in the finest restaurants. Additionally, since it is cooked for 2 hours, most of the fat drips off, making the Peking Duck very lean indeed. The best season to make this dish is winter when the air is dry and cold.

    1 duckling, 5 to 6 pounds
    2 tablespoons sugar
    2 tablespoons boiling water
    4 tablespoons hoisin sauce
      Thin Cakes (p.55) or
      Steamed Buns (p.99)
      Scallion Brushes (p. 132)

Bring 2 quarts water to boil in a wok. ② Scald one side of duck until color changes. Turn and repeat. Drain and set on platter.

Mix sugar with boiling water. Stir until the solution is clear. ③ Brush over the duck skin. ④ With a sharp knife, cut a hole in the tail. Thread it with a string. ⑤ Hang duck by the tail in a cool, airy place until the skin is dry, about 12 to 24 hours. An electric fan will speed up the process.

Preheat oven to 400°F. Place duck backside up on rack in roasting pan*. Roast for 30 minutes. Turn heat to 250°F and roast for 50 to 60 minutes. Turn breast side up, turn heat to 400°F again, roast for another 30 minutes. Carve duck and place on a platter. Or you may choose to carve at the table. Let each person serve himself by placing a piece of meat and a piece of skin in a Thin Cake, then brushing it with hoisin sauce using the Scallion Brush. Roll up everything, including the Scallion Brush, into a neat roll. Make sandwiches with Steamed Buns if they are served.

*You may also stand the duck on a vertical duck roaster. Bake it at the same temperatures as above. No turning is necessary.

叉燒肉

Chinese Barbecued Pork

Barbecued Pork, or Char Siu, *(Cantonese pronunciation for* 叉燒*), is a common sight in a Chinese grocery store. Strips of reddish meat are seen hanging on hooks behind glass windows. This delightful dish can be bought from the store or prepared at home. It is used in many different ways: a main dish or an appetizer, served hot or cold; filling for* Bao *or garnish for soups; ingredient for Stir-Frying with bean curd and other vegetables. I usually make several pounds at a time and freeze part of it.*

The following is a traditional recipe adapted to the American kitchen. To avoid using food coloring, I combine gin and light soy sauce to create a reddish look.

    2 pounds pork, loin or butt

Marinade
    ½ teaspoon salt
    2 tablespoons hoisin sauce
    4 tablespoons light soy sauce
    1 tablespoon gin

Cut pork into 1" x 2" x 6" strips. Combine with **Marinade** and refrigerate for 6 hours or overnight. Turn occasionally.

Use only one oven rack and place it in the highest position. Place a large pan filled with one inch of water on the floor of the oven to catch drippings.

② Make hooks by opening paper clips. ③ Hook pork strips to the oven rack. You may do this before the oven is turned on. Turn the oven to 400°F. Bake until crusty brown, about 45 to 50 minutes. Don't overcook. Look in occasionally to make sure nothing is burning. ④ Cut into strips. Serve hot or cold. May be refrigerated for several days or frozen indefinitely.

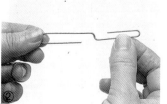

烤排骨

Chinese Barbecued Spareribs

My students love to nibble on these tasty spareribs. I think you will enjoy them, too.

> 1 slab small-bone spareribs
> (about 2 pounds)

Marinade
> 3 cloves garlic
> 2 fresh chilies (optional)
> ¼ teaspoon five-spice powder
> 2 tablespoons hoisin sauce
> 2 tablespoons catsup
> 4 tablespoons light soy sauce
> 1 tablespoon gin (yes, you read it right!)
> 1 teaspoon honey

Ask the butcher to cut across ribs twice. Cut the long strips into 5 to 6-inch pieces for easy handling. Crush garlic. Chop chilies and discard seeds. Combine with the rest of the **Marinade** and rub on the ribs. Refrigerate for 6 hours or overnight. Turn occasionally.

Use only one oven rack and place it in the highest position. Place a large pan filled with one inch of water on the floor of the oven to catch drippings.

② Make hooks by opening paper clips. ③ Hook ribs to the oven rack before the oven is turned on. Turn the oven to 400°F. Bake until crusty, about 40 to 45 minutes. Check occasionally to see that the ribs are not charred. Remove immediately. Don't overcook. When cool enough to handle, separate the ribs. Serve hot or cold.

①

烤肉捲

Baked Pork Rolls

There are not many Chinese dishes cooked in the oven because it is not part of the Chinese kitchen. I have developed this recipe especially for Americans who like to use the oven. The slightly sweet rolls with crunchy center are perfect either as a main dish or as an appetizer.

1 pound pork tenderloin

Marinade
1 teaspoon cornstarch
1 tablespoon sugar
⅛ teaspoon pepper
2 tablespoons soy sauce
2 tablespoons ketchup
1 tablespoon wine
1 tablespoon vinegar
1 teaspoon sesame oil

Stuffing
6 dried mushrooms
8 water chestnuts
4 whole scallions

12 toothpicks

Preheat oven to 400°F. Cut tenderloin crosswise into 12 thin slices. (Partially frozen meat is easier to cut.) Pound with a mallet or back of cleaver in a crisscross fashion. Combine with **Marinade** and let stand for 15 minutes.

Soak mushrooms in warm water for 15 minutes. Discard water and stems. Shred mushrooms, water chestnuts and scallions. ② Roll ½ of **Stuffing** in each slice of pork. Fasten with a toothpick. Arrange rolls in a single layer in a baking dish. Pour excess **Marinade** over. Bake at 400°F oven for 20 minutes. *May be prepared ahead, refrigerated or frozen and re-heated.*

If served as an appetizer, cut each roll into 4 pieces. Serve cold on toothpicks.

燒餅

Shaobing

Makes 24 pieces of pastry.

Shaobing, *served with hot soy bean milk, is a popular breakfast dish of the Chinese. The pastry can be made either with Yeast Dough or Fluffy Pastry Dough (p.108). The following recipe uses Yeast Dough.*

    1 recipe Yeast Dough (p.132) *

Filling
    2 cups chopped scallions, with
      mostly green part
    ½ cup margarine
    1 teaspoon salt

    ½ cup sesame seeds

*Substitute 4 packages refrigerated biscuit dough. No need for the second rising. Follow baking instructions on package.

Mince **filling** ingredients together. This will reduce the volume to less than 1 cup. Roll dough into a long stick. Cut into 24 portions. Shape each into a patty. ② Roll with one hand and rotate with the other into a disc 2½″ in diameter, with the edge thinner than the center. Place 1 tablespoon of **Filling** on each patty. Don't overfill. ③ Gather the edges. Pinch to seal. Flatten by pressing with fingers. ④ Press into sesame seeds. Place the side with seeds up on a tray, apart from each other. Cover with cloth and let rise again for 30 minutes. Set apart on an ungreased cookie sheet. Bake at 375°F until brown, about 12 minutes.

芝麻小餅
Sesame Cookies

Makes 36 cookies

Here is a Chinese dessert which is not soupy, and which does not have to be fried at the last minute. You can serve something delicate, fragrant, light and crunchy which complements American sherbert just as well as it does Chinese Almond Doufu. It will certainly bring you many compliments. Eat it in good health!

Flour Mixture
- 1½ cups cake flour
- 1 teaspoon baking powder
- ¼ teaspoon salt

- ½ cup sugar
- ½ cup shortening
- 1 egg
- 1 teaspoon vanilla
- ¼ cup white sesame seeds

Combine **Flour Mixture** and set aside. Stir the sugar and shortening. Add egg, vanilla and stir again. Add **Flour Mixture** and knead until an even, soft dough is formed. Roll into two logs, each 6 inches long. Wrap in wax paper and refrigerate for 6 hours or overnight.

Pre-heat oven to 350°F. With a sharp knife, slice the logs into circles ¼″ thick. Press each circle in the sesame seeds. Lay it on a greased cookie sheet with the sesame side up, apart from others. Bake at 350°F until golden brown, about 10 to 12 minutes. Transfer onto a platter to cool.

桃酥
Walnut Cookies

Makes 32 cookies

This is one of my father's stories that I enjoy very much:

"Once there was a lazy man whose wife was going away. Worried that her husband might die of starvation, she baked a huge cookie and hung it around his neck. Upon returning, the poor woman found her husband dead. He had eaten the front part of the cookie but did not bother to turn it around."

Too bad she did not use the following recipe. It could have saved the man's life because it so good that even the laziest person would have turned it around!

Flour Mixture
- 3 cups sifted flour
- ½ teaspoon baking soda
- ½ teaspoon baking powder
- ¼ teaspoon salt

- 1½ cups butter or shortening
- ½ egg, beaten
- ¾ cup white sugar
- 1 tablespoon dark corn syrup
- 1 teaspoon vanilla extract
- 32 walnut halves

Preheat oven to 350°F.

Sift **Flour Mixture** and set aside.

Thoroughly mix butter, eggs and sugar. Add corn syrup and vanilla. Mix again. Gradually pour into **Flour Mixture**; mix with a fork as one would do for pie crust until a crumbly dough is formed. **Do Not Over-handle and Do Not Use A Food Processor.** Squeeze gently into 32 balls. ② Flatten each ball by pressing in a walnut half. (Don't worry if they are not round.) Set cookies on a cookie sheet apart from each other. Bake until golden brown, about 10 minutes.

Other Applications
Almond Cookies: Substitute almond extract for vanilla extract; substitute almonds for walnuts.

棗泥酥餅
Jujube Fluffy Pastry

Makes 8 pastries.

This pastry is made of the following Fluffy Pastry Dough, from which most Chinese pastries are made. If you don't want to make the dough, use frozen puff pastry.

Water Dough *
- 1 cup cake flour
- 1 teaspoon sugar
- 2 tablespoons vegetable oil
- 3 tablespoons water

Lard Dough *
- ½ cup cake flour
- 3 tablespoons lard, butter or margarine

Filling
- ½ cup jujube paste **
- ¼ cup chopped walnuts
- 2 tablespoons lard, butter or margarine
- 1 tablespoon cornstarch

- 1 egg yolk, beaten w/1 tablespoon water

*Substitute one 17-oz. package frozen puff pastry for the above dough. Follow baking instructions on package.

**Buy in cans or make at home: Soak 1 cup jujubes in warm water for 30 minutes. Drain. Simmer in 1 cup water until liquid is absorbed. De-pit and mince when cool.

Knead **Water Dough** and **Lard Dough** separately. Work with half of each dough first. ② Roll out **Water Dough**. Spread **Lard Dough** over it. Fold in thirds into a rectangle. ③ Fold the two ends toward the center into a square. Roll out. Don't worry if dough breaks. Sprinkle flour if necessary. Repeat the folding and rolling 3 times. Finally roll out into 8″ square. ④ Cut into 4 equal squares.

Mix **Filling** ingredients well. ⑤ Place ⅛ of it on a square. Fold over diagonally. Pinch edges to seal. Trim edges. ⑥ Press edges with a fork. Brush with egg yolk mixture. Place on an ungreased cookie sheet. Cover with waxed paper and let rest for 10 minutes. Repeat with the other half of the dough.

Preheat oven to 425°F. Bake the pastry — leaving the waxed paper on — for 10 minutes. Turn heat down to 325°F and bake for 15 minutes. Remove paper when cooked.

Other Applications:
Date Fluffy Pastry: Substitute ½ cup pitted dates for jujube paste. Mince. Omit cornstarch in **Filling**.

CURING METHOD 醃

Curing was the principal method of preserving meat and fish before the invention of refrigerators. Today it is still widely used because cured food is different from fresh food, firmer in texture and stronger in taste. Furthermore, it keeps for a long time and requires no last-minute hassle.

The first step in Curing is *Salting* 醃 , in which meat, poultry or fish are marinated in salt for a period of time until a change takes place: the texture becomes firmer, and the taste spicier.

In today's kitchen, marinated meat is wrapped in plastic bags and left in the refrigerator for days; afterwards it is rinsed and steamed or simmered. Then it can be chopped and served, as in the case of Salted Fish; or it can be further smoked as in the case of Smoked Fish.

Smoking, 燻 , means applying smoke to salted food. Traditionally, the food is hung in an outdoor oven, and smoked by burning sawdust, peanut shells, pine needles and spices. Raw smoked food is steamed before serving. It can also be used to season other food. Hunan, my parents' home province, is famous for smoked bacon. Each year, at winter solstice, my grandmother would have pigs slaughtered. They were first offered to the gods, to the spirits of the ancestors, and then to the guests at the feast. Servants would be busy for days making bacon, ham and sausages. The smoked bacon would last all year long.

In today's kitchen, Smoking is done in a wok as follows: ① Line bottom of wok with foil. Spread brown sugar on it. Place a cake rack over sugar. ② Place the food to be smoked on rack, breast side up if a bird is smoked. The food should not have direct contact with sugar. Cover. ③ Stuff the crevices with damp paper towels to keep the smoke in.

Turn heat to medium. You should be able to smell the smoke after two minutes; otherwise turn heat higher. After 10 minutes, turn off heat, but do not open the cover for another 10 minutes. Now the food is smoked.

Frequent smoking takes away the seasoning of the wok. Therefore, it is necessary to rub it with oil or even re-season it after smoking.

The smoking can also be done on a cook-out grill, with the foil directly laid on the charcoal and the food placed on the grate. In the case of flat fish, you can cook and smoke it at the same time, thus skipping the step of Steaming. Dripping fat tends to cause the fire to flare up and burn the food. Therefore, fatty food such as ducks and spareribs should not be smoked on a cook-out grill.

Wining, 醉 , is marinating poultry or seafood in wine, salt and spices. Live crabs and shrimp are literally drowned in alcohol and eaten raw. I don't like to force alcohol on these unwilling victims. Therefore, I only use the recipe for Drunken Chicken, in which the bird is killed, cooked, and *then* marinated in wine.

灯籠鶏

Lantern Chicken

Lantern festival falls on the 15th day of the first month of the lunar calendar. It marks the last day of the New Year celebrations. Riddles are written on the sides of the lantern, and the one who gets the right answer wins a prize. Somewhat similar to the Halloween observance, the lantern festival is also a children's festival. They prefer to walk in the darkest alleys, so that they may show off the bright light of their lanterns. This dish is called lantern chicken because the chicken's red color reminds one of the bright red lantern. Spicy and festive, yet simple to make, this dish is served as an appetizer or main dish.

    1 chicken

Marinade
    3 slices ginger
    2 whole scallions
    1 tablespoon Sichuan peppercorn
    3 tablespoons salt
_____
    2 tablespoons chili powder, divided*
    1 tablespoon sesame oil

*Substitute paprika for part of the chili powder if you prefer a milder taste.

Smash ginger and scallions with side of cleaver. Cut scallion into sections, combine with the rest of **Marinade** and rub it on chicken, inside and out. Wrap in plastic bag and leave in the refrigerator for 1 day. Rinse in cold water. Scald in boiling water for 2 minutes. Smear half of chili powder over the skin.

Bring water in steamer to boil. Steam chicken over high flame for 45 minutes. Discard liquid. Rub the remaining chili powder over the skin. Serve hot or cold, either chopped (p.12) or carved at the table like any other roasted bird.

燻 鷄
Smoked Chicken

There are not many Chinese dishes that you can bring to a picnic or a potluck supper. This recipe is an exception, and it is exceptionally popular with both Chinese and Americans. It can be used either as a main dish or as an appetizer.

　　1 roaster, 3 to 4 pounds

Marinade
　　3 tablespoons salt
　　1 tablespoon Sichuan peppercorn

　　¼ cup brown sugar
　　　some sesame oil

Rub chicken with **Marinade**, inside and out. Place in a plastic bag, with breast side down. Pile excess **Marinade** in the cavity over the thick part of the breast and the thighs. Close the bag and place it inside another bag to prevent leakage. Place in the refrigerator for 3 days.

Bring water in steamer to boil. Rinse chicken thoroughly. Place it in a large bowl, breast side up. Set the bowl in the steamer. Cover steamer and steam for 45 minutes. Drain and discard liquid.

Follow instructions on p. 109 to smoke the chicken. Transfer the chicken to a plate. ② Brush the skin with sesame oil. When cooled, chop into 1″ × 3″ strips, and arrange on serving platter (p. 12.) If you prefer to serve the chicken on toothpicks, bone it and cube it into bite-sized pieces. Serve cold. Can be kept in the refrigerator for two weeks.

Other Applications
Smoked Turkey: Use a large steamer and a cook-out grill. Substitute the smallest turkey you can find for the chicken. Use 1 tablespoon salt and 1 teaspoon Sichuan peppercorn per pound of turkey. Marinate for a week. Steam for 2 hours. Smoke by putting brown sugar on foil directly placed on the charcoal, and lay the bird on the grill, breast side up. The fire should not be too high. This will continue to cook and smoke at the same time. Check occasionally to see that the turkey is thoroughly cooked and the skin is brown. Brush with sesame oil. May be carved at the table. Great for a buffet.

燻排骨

Smoked Spareribs

If you like to nibble on bones as the Chinese do, you will enjoy this flavorful dish. To do justice to the spareribs, you must have a glass of good wine.

    1 slab spareribs, 2 to 3 pounds

Marinade
    3 fresh red chilies
    3 slices ginger, shredded
    2 whole scallions, shredded
    2 tablespoons salt
    1 tablespoon Sichuan peppercorn
    3 tablespoons wine rice (p.132)

    ¼ cup brown sugar
    2 tablespoons red tea

Ask the butcher to cut through the spareribs twice across the bones, but not to separate the ribs.

De-seed chilies. Rinse under water unless you like it very hot. Shred. Combine all **Marinade** ingredients and mix with ribs. Wrap in a double plastic bag and refrigerate for 2 days.

Bring water in steamer to boil. Set ribs in a bowl in the steamer and steam over high flame for 45 minutes. Discard liquid and the solid **Marinade** that is sticking to the ribs.

Smoke with brown sugar and tea; follow instructions on p. 109. Don't brush with sesame oil. Cut ribs apart and serve cold. Can be refrigerated for weeks.

Other Applications
Salt and Pepper Spareribs: After steaming, separate ribs, spread on tray to dry for one hour. Deep-Fry in 350°F oil until brown. Serve with Salt and Pepper Dip (p.130).

燻魚

Smoked Fish

I did not smoke fish much until we lived on the West Coast. I was most delighted with the variety of fresh fish that can be smoked in the states of Washington and California. Of all the fish found on the West Coast, the small salmon is my favorite for smoking.

    1 fish, 1½ to 2 pounds *

Marinade
    3 slices ginger
    2 whole scallions
    1 tablespoon salt
    1 tablespoon Sichuan peppercorn
    1 tablespoon wine

    ¼ cup brown sugar
    sesame oil

*Any kind with firm meat

Have the fish salesperson clean the fish. Leave the head and tail on. Make slashes across the body of the fish 1″ apart. Smash ginger and scallions with side of cleaver. Cut scallions into sections. Combine **Marinade** and rub over fish, inside, outside, and between slashes. Place in the refrigerator in plastic bag for 1 day.

Bring water in the steamer to boil. Rinse fish and place on a heat-proof platter, and set in the steamer. Steam for 10 to 15 minutes.

Follow instructions on p. 109 and smoke the fish. Serve cold: whole or cut up. If using cook-out grill for smoking, you may skip steaming, but prolong the smoking time.

Other Applications
Smoked Fish Steaks: Substitute 1½ pound fish steak for fish; leave the skin on.

Quick-Cured Fish: Use any flat fish. Make slashes very deep. Salt for 1 hour instead of 1 day. Steam and smoke as above.

Salted Fish: Use the same ingredients and follow the same steps as **Smoked Fish**, but omit the process of Smoking.

醉 鷄

Drunken Chicken

The chicken is not drunk, it is just marinated in wine. I can't guarantee that this delicious bird will not get you intoxicated, particularly if you serve a good wine with it!

½ roaster or 2 whole chicken breasts

Marinade
  2 whole scallions
  3 slices ginger
  1 tablespoon salt

  ¾ cup Shaohsing wine
  1 stalk fresh coriander

Smash scallion and ginger with side of cleaver. Cut scallions into sections. Combine **Marinade** and rub over chicken. Let stand for 1 hour.

Place chicken in a snug-fitting pot with **Marinade.** Add just enough water to cover the chicken. Bring to boil over high heat. Turn heat off. Let chicken stay in the liquid, covered, for 10 minutes. Repeat once. (Twice if you want it well-done, but not as tender.) Drain and cool. Reserve liquid.

Cut chicken into 1″ strips. (The Chinese like to nibble on bones; but if you prefer to serve it on toothpicks, bone and cut the chicken into bite-sized pieces.) Place chicken in a bowl, with meaty part on the bottom, skin-side down. Fill the bowl with the bony pieces. Pour over wine mixed with 1 cup of reserved liquid. Add more liquid to cover chicken. (The excess liquid can be used as broth for other dishes.) Cover and refrigerate for 1 day.

Pour off liquid and set aside. Cover bowl with platter and invert. Pour liquid over. Serve cold. *The dish may be kept in the liquid in the refrigerator for a week. The liquid can be frozen and used again. Use much less wine on subsequent uses.*

PICKLING METHOD 泡

Pickling, 泡 , is marinating vegetables in sugar, salt, vinegar and spices. Often salt is mixed with the vegetable first. The moisture drawn out by the salt is discarded, which makes the pickle extra crunchy.

The Cantonese pickle food with sugar and vinegar, the Northerners with lots of garlic, and the Sichuanese add chili, ginger, and Sichuan peppercorn. In most parts of China, pungent pickles are served with bland rice porridge. They are also used as side dishes for lunch and supper.

Pickles are said to "go with rice," which means that they help the rice go down smoothly. They are essential for the Chinese who use rice as a staple. The plentiful supply of a wide variety of food in recent years has diminished the importance of rice to some extent. However, pickles sure are refreshing after a long succession of rich dishes.

In some restaurants, various pickles are brought out in small plates on a tray, so that the customers may nibble on them while making up their minds as to what they want to order.

10. PICKLING DEMONSTRATION RECIPES

廣東泡菜

Cantonese Pickles (Bottom Picture)

This dish is sweet, sour and crunchy. It tastes particularly refreshing after a rich meal. The Cantonese also use these pickles in sweet and sour dishes. I usually make several recipes of this dish and keep them in the refrigerator.

Vegetables
- 2 carrots
- ½ icicle radish
- 2 gherkin cucumbers

- 1 teaspoon salt

Seasoning
- 1 chili
- 3 thin slices ginger
- 3 tablespoons sugar
- 3 tablespoons vinegar

Peel carrots. Scrub icicle radish and cucumbers but leave skin on. ② Roll-cut **Vegetables** into 3 cups. Mix with 1 teaspoon salt and let them stand at room temperature for 4 to 6 hours. Stir occasionally. Drain. Squeeze out and discard excess liquid in vegetables.

③ Cut across chili to make little rings. Rinse in cold water to make less hot because Cantonese dishes are never very spicy. Combine with the rest of the **Seasoning** and **Vegetables.**

Chill in refrigerator for 6 hours or overnight. Stir occasionally. May be kept in refrigerator for several weeks.

四川泡菜

Sichuan Pickled Vegetables

The pickle urn, with the ingenious design of a canal around its neck to keep it airtight, brings back memories of being a little girl growing up in Sichuan Province. You, too, can enjoy this delicacy. Use a large, airtight jar to keep these vegetables. You add vinegar to give the pickles the sour taste which the natural fermentation in the urn used to produce.

Marinade
- 4 teaspoons salt
- 2 tablespoons sugar
- 1 tablespoon Sichuan peppercorn
- 2 tablespoons wine
- 2 tablespoons vinegar
- 2 cups water
- 3 to 5 whole chilies, fresh or dried
- 3 cloves garlic (unpeeled)

Vegetables

- Chinese cabbage stems
- cabbage
- carrots
- icicle radishes
- gherkin cucumbers

Combine **Marinade** in an airtight quart-sized jar. It must be absolutely clean, free of grease. Mix **Marinade** ingredients thoroughly.

Select any number of **Vegetables** from list. Prepare them as follows:

Wash Chinese cabbage stems and cut into lengthwise strips. Wash cabbage and cut into wedges. Peel carrots and cut into strips. Scrub icicle radishes and gherkin cucumbers. Don't peel them. Cut into strips.

Immerse **Vegetables** of your choice in **Marinade.** Close the jar tightly and leave in the refrigerator for a day. Enjoy your pickles from now on. Add more **Vegetables** and **Marinade** when the jar gets low. Vegetables can be kept in the refrigerator for months, if someone doesn't eat them all first!

麻辣黄瓜

Tangy Peppery Cucumbers

The principle of yin (the feminine, the cold, the dark) and yang (the masculine, the hot, the bright) governs the entire span of Chinese life. When yin and yang are in harmony, the world functions the way it should. The culinary arts observe the principle of yin and yang as a matter of course. For instance, in this dish, cucumbers are yin; eating too many will cause a stomach ache. Counteract the yin with chili pepper, which is yang. Not surprisingly, well-balanced yin and yang, such as sweet and tender gherkin cucumbers (yin) and hot and harsh chili (yang), provide a good contrast in both taste and color.

- 1 pound gherkin cucumbers ·
- 1 teaspoon salt

Seasoning
- 1 fresh red chili*
- 3 cloves garlic
- 1 tablespoon sugar
- ½ teaspoon Sichuan peppercorn

Sesame oil

*Add more to taste

Wash and scrub cucumbers with a dish cloth. Roll-cut (p. 9). Mix with salt and let stand for 1 hour. Drain and discard liquid.

Slice chili diagonally. Discard seeds. Smash garlic with side of cleaver. Combine with the rest of **Seasoning** ingredients and mix with cucumbers. Cover and chill in refrigerator for 2 hours. *May be kept in the refrigerator for weeks.* Sprinkle with sesame oil before serving.

酸辣白菜

Sour Hot Celery Cabbage

The Chinese have been making pickles for centuries. The Chou Dynasty (1122?-256?B.C.) records indicate that sixty-two pickle and sauce specialists were employed in the Imperial Kitchens. Under the Tang Dynasty (618-906 A.D.), pickling became a highly developed culinary art.

- 1½ pounds Chinese cabbage
- 2 tablespoons oil
- 1 teaspoon Sichuan peppercorn
- 3 dried chilies

Seasoning
- 1 teaspoon salt
- 3 tablespoons sugar
- 4 tablespoons vinegar
- 3 tablespoons light soy sauce

- 1 teaspoon sesame oil

Wash cabbage and drain. Cut across into 2" sections. Separate leaves from the stems. Combine **Seasoning**.

Heat 2 tablespoons oil in wok until almost smoking. Fry peppercorn until fragrant. ② Remove as many peppercorns as you can and discard. *Be careful because they pop up occasionally.* ③ Add chilies to the pepper-flavored oil and fry until black. Stir in cabbage until wilted. (Turn heat lower if the cabbage has a tendency to burn.) Add **Seasoning.** When it boils, transfer into a bowl, cover and refrigerate for 6 hours. *May be kept in the refrigerator for weeks.* Before serving, drain and mix with sesame oil.

①

②

③

COLD-MIXING METHOD 涼拌

Cold-Mixing, 涼拌 , is the method used to make Chinese salads. Leafy vegetables are blanched first, and then plunged into cold water to cool. The process abruptly interrupts the cooking. This enables the green vegetables to retain their color and crispness. Fruit and root vegetables, such as cucumbers, carrots, and icicle radishes are used raw: salted first to draw out excess moisture so that they will taste crisp. Other items, such as seafood, poultry, meat, as well as noodles, are fully cooked first. Jellyfish, agar-agar, bean curd, bean threads, and bean sheets are also familiar salad ingredients.

The dressing is usually mixed with food just before serving, particularly with leafy vegetables. The most common salad dressing is a combination of soy sauce, vinegar, sugar and sesame oil. Sesame paste is often used on noodles or chicken meat. The Cantonese like to add oyster sauce to their Cold-Mixed dishes. The Shangdung folks use lots of garlic, but rarely any sugar. The Sichuanese use chili pepper and Sichuan peppercorn in addition to a host of other spices.

Jellying, 凍 , can be used to make both sweet and savory dishes. In China, agar-agar is used for Jellying. However, unflavored gelatin is readily available and easy to use. The gelatin dishes taste just like those made of agar-agar do, but the latter are firmer in texture.

Always include some Cold-Mixed dishes in your menu when you entertain. This serves to calm your nerves because you are assured that at least some dishes are already prepared.

担担麵

The Peddler's Noodles

Dan Dan Mien, or the Peddler's Noodles, originated in a little alley in the City of Chungking. The dish became popular and soon there were hundreds of peddlers all over the streets shouting "Dan Dan Mien." As a young girl, I used to love this little treat. When I returned to Chungking after an absence of 35 years, my schoolmates wanted to know if there was anything special that I cared for. I told them: "Dan Dan Mien." I found that the noodles and garnish were still familiar; but they had added broth and meat sauce to it. Food, like a living language, is forever changing. The following recipe is faithful to the original, which is very good and nourishing.

    1 pound fine noodles*
    1 tablespoon oil

Garnish
    ¼ cup *jahtsai*
    ¼ cup Tientsin preserved vegetables
    ¼ cup roasted skinless peanuts
    4 whole scallions
    3 tablespoons sesame paste
    4 tablespoons water

    light soy sauce
    sesame oil
    chili oil

*Buy the finest noodles you can find. Chances are that you can get only dry noodles of the fine variety.

Bring a large pot of water to boil. Boil noodles until cooked. Drain and mix with 1 tablespoon oil. Spread on plates to cool. Place on a large platter and set on table.

Prepare **Garnish** as follows, and place each ingredient in a separate bowl on the table. Chop the first 4 ingredients as fine as you can. Add 4 tablespoons water to sesame paste, a little at a time, stirring while mixing, until a thin smooth paste is formed.

Set a bowl and a pair of chopsticks for each person. Let him or her fill the bowl with noodles half full, then garnish with ingredients of his choice. Everything can be prepared ahead of time. You can serve this dish also on a huge platter, already assembled with noodles at the bottom and **Garnish** on top. Use proportionately less **Garnish** when serving on one platter.

11. COLD-MIXING DEMONSTRATION RECIPES

銀芽鷄絲

Silver Chicken Threads

This elegant salad stands out from the rest by its aristocratic appearance and subtle taste. Agar-agar is a seaweed, high in nutrition and low in calories. This can also be said of the two other ingredients: chicken breast and bean sprouts. Who says good-tasting food has to be high in calories? A good dish for home, it is also fine for picnics and potlucks.

    1 whole chicken breast or
      2 cups leftover breast meat
    1 ounce agar-agar
    8 ounces bean sprouts

Seasoning
    ½ teaspoon salt
    1 teaspoon chicken bouillon powder
    2 teaspoons sugar
    2 teaspoons vinegar
    ¼ teaspoon ginger juice
    1 teaspoon chili oil (optional)
    1 tablespoon sesame oil

Place chicken breasts in a pot, add just enough water to cover. Bring water to boil. Turn heat off and leave chicken in the covered pot for 8 minutes. Repeat. Drain. Reserve broth for other dishes. Discard skin and bone. Shred the meat by tearing with fingers.

Bring a large pot of water to boil. Dip agar-agar in water. ② Immediately lift it out and plunge it into cold water. Drain. Do it quickly, otherwise agar-agar will melt. Cut across it a few times.

Keep the pot of water boiling. Pour in bean sprouts. When the water boils again, drain and plunge bean sprouts into cold water. Change water until they are chilled.

Combine chicken, agar agar, and bean sprouts on serving platter; put **Seasoning** in a bowl. Chill both in refrigerator for at least one hour. Just before serving, pour **Seasoning** over chicken. Mix at the table.

涼拌黃瓜

Cold-Mixed Cucumbers

This crispy salad should have a light green appearance, so don't spoil the looks with any soy sauce. Chili oil adds excitement to the dish. Select cucumbers that are bumpy. By the time they grow to be smooth, they are too old.

    2 to 3 cucumbers *
    ½ teaspoon salt

Dressing
    1 teaspoon sugar
    1 teaspoon vinegar
    1 teaspoon sesame oil
    1 teaspoon chili oil (optional)

*Gherkin cucumbers are best. They are hard to find. If you do find them, do not peel the skin. Cut diagonally into oval-shaped slices.

Peel cucumbers. Split lengthwise into halves. Scoop out seeds with a spoon and discard. Cut across into ¼" slices. Mix with ½ teaspoon salt and let stand for 20 minutes. Drain and discard liquid.

Combine with **Dressing** and serve cold or at room temperature.

Other Applications
Cold-Mixed Icicle Radishes: Substitute 1 icicle radish for cucumbers. Peel and shred. Add 1 whole scallion, shredded.

懷油芥蘭

Chinese Broccoli in Oyster Sauce

A favorite recipe of mine for parties, not only because it looks beautiful and tastes good, but also because there is no last-minute rush.

1 pound Chinese broccoli

Dressing
a pinch of salt
1 teaspoon sugar
1 tablespoon oyster sauce
1 tablespoon thick soy sauce
1 teaspoon sesame oil
1 tablespoon broth or water

Peel broccoli stems. Scald in large pot of boiling water for 1 minute. Cool in cold water immediately. Squeeze out excess water. Arrange in one direction. ② Cut across 2 or 3 times. Transfer onto platter. Pour **Dressing** over just before serving.

Other Applications
Broccoli in Oyster Sauce: Substitute broccoli for Chinese broccoli. Separate florets from stem. Peel stem and slice lengthwise into pieces 2″ long. Cut florets lengthwise if large.

Asparagus in Oyster Sauce: Substitute asparagus for Chinese broccoli. Use only the tender tips. Cut across 2 or 3 times.

Cold Celery Slices: Substitute a head of celery for Chinese broccoli. Slice diagonally. Substitute 1 to 3 teaspoons chili oil for oyster sauce and add a pinch of m.s.g.

Cold-Mixed String Beans: Substitute 1 pound string beans for Chinese broccoli. String. Boil until tender. Substitute 1 teaspoon chili oil for oyster sauce.

黑白豆腐

Black and White Doufu

Some people call the preserved duck eggs "Thousand-year-old Eggs." If you are too chicken to eat the exaggerated egg, omit the obvious exaggeration, and call the dish: "Bean Curd Salad," or "Doufu Salad." The Chinese eat Bean Curd Salad with rice porridge for breakfast. My students make sandwiches out of the salad, or spread it on crackers.

1 pound bean curd

Dressing
¼ teaspoon salt
1 teaspoon sugar
2 teaspoons vinegar
1 tablespoon soy sauce
1 teaspoon sesame oil
1 whole scallion, chopped

1 preserved duck egg
1 stalk fresh coriander

Set bean curd on plate for 15 minutes to drain. Transfer to serving plate. Pour over **Dressing**. Peel preserved eggs and cut into halves. Top bean curd with egg. Decorate with fresh coriander. Mix at the table.

Other Applications
Cold-Mixed Pressed Bean Curd: Substitute ½ pound pressed bean curd for bean curd. Omit salt, m.s.g. and duck egg. Shred before mixing.

杏仁豆腐
Almond Doufu

This delicate, almond flavored ivory custard has the appearance of doufu, bean curd, so it is called Almond Doufu. Fruity, cool, light and refreshing, it is a perfect dessert for the summertime. The following recipe uses unflavored gelatin. For the strict vegetarian, see the agar-agar method below. Although made of different jelling agents, the two dishes taste and look alike, except that the agar-agar dish is firmer in texture.

Almond Dofu
- 3 cups boiling water
- ¾ cup sugar
- 2 packages unflavored gelatin
- 1 13 oz. can evaporated milk
- 1 tablespoon almond extract

Syrup
- 3 cups hot water
- 6 tablespoons sugar
- 2 teaspoons almond extract

- 1 15 oz. can Oriental fruit, chilled*

*Fresh strawberries, canned pineapple, mandarin oranges, lichees, and cherries can also be used.

Dissolve sugar and gelatin in boiling water. Add milk. Pour into an 8″ x 13″ cake pan. Cool to lukewarm and add 1 tablespoon almond extract. When completely cool, cover and refrigerate for at least 6 hours or overnight. ① Cut into ¾″ squares.

Make **Syrup** by dissolving 6 tablespoons sugar in 3 cups hot water. Add 2 teaspoons almond extract when cool. Chill in the refrigerator.

② Carefully pour **Syrup** in **Almond Doufu**. The squares should float. Gently pour into a soup tureen. Garnish with chilled fruit. May be prepared ahead and kept in the refrigerator for a week.

Other Applications:
Agar-Agar Method: Substitute ½ oz. agar-agar for unflavored gelatin. Soak in cold water for 1 minute. Drain and simmer in 3 cups water for 15 minutes. Add milk and cool to lukewarm. Follow the rest of the steps as given above.

琵琶凍
Loquat Mold

Loquat, 琵琶, is a soft-textured, delicate tasting, teardrop-shaped Oriental fruit. Because of its soft texture, either the fresh or canned variety can be used in this recipe, which demonstrates how you can use various fruits to make Oriental fruit mold.

- 1 cup boiling water
- ¼ cup sugar
- 1 package unflavored gelatin
- ½ cup juice from canned loquat
- 1 16 oz. can loquat
  maraschino cherries

Dissolve sugar and gelatin in boiling water. Add mixture to loquat juice. Chill until thick, but not yet set.

In a shallow bowl, arrange loquat and cherries in an attractive pattern. Pour gelatin mixture over. Cover and refrigerate for 6 hours or more.

Set the bowl in warm water for 2 minutes. Invert it onto a serving platter. May be prepared ahead of time and refrigerated for a week.

Other Applications:
Try various canned fruit: Tangerines, lichees, pineapples, etc. Decorate with candied fruit. Flavored gelatin with the same flavor as the fruit can also be used. Follow instructions on package.

七星併盤

Seven-Star Platter

This is a very festive dish, often used as the first course of a banquet. You can also use it at a cocktail party, placing only finger food on the platter. Restaurants use a platter specifically made for this dish. It has 7 compartments. For family cooking, use a huge platter, or a round tray lined with foil. Watch how the eyes of your **guests light up in pleasure!**

Candied Walnuts
Salted Duck, chopped
Lu Beef, sliced
Smoked Chicken, chopped
Boiled Ham, sliced
Pseudo Smoked Fish
Cantonese Pickles

Set walnuts in the center. Arrange everything around the nuts.

Create your own seven stars, using anything chosen from the Cold-Mixed, Cured, Pickled categories. Or you may choose anything from any category that can be served conveniently. If you don't mind last-minute hassle, include fried items, such as Shrimp Toast or Puffed Shrimp Balls.

AUXILIARY METHODS

The primary cooking methods are complete methods to cook food. However, additional methods to prepare and cook food are sometimes necessary. These are supportive or auxiliary methods which are not sufficient cooking methods in themselves.

BLANCHING: Can be done either in water or oil.

Water-Blanching, 燙 : Scald the vegetables in rolling boiling water first, and then plunge into cold water to chill. The scalding takes away the raw taste; the abrupt interruption of cooking preserves the green color and crispy texture. Many cold-mixed vegetables are prepared this way (Chinese Broccoli in Oyster Sauce).

Meats and poultry are also blanched in boiling water, and then rinsed in cold water to remove residue, so that the broth will come out clear.

Oil-Blanching, 過油 : Passing meat, poultry, sea food and vegetables through hot or warm oil before final Stir-Frying. The oil must not be so hot as to brown the meat. Dishes cooked this way are more brilliant in appearance and softer in texture (Gung Bao Chicken). It is different from Deep-Frying, a process which fully cooks the meat.

Most Chinese restaurants apply Oil-Blanching prior to Stir-Frying. Overseas Chinese restaurants often have a pot of oil simmering all the time just for this purpose. The method is rarely used in home-cooking, except for Stir-Fried fish (Fish Slices in Wine Sauce). Most fish disintegrates when stirred like meat; Oil-Blanching enables it to keep its shape.

INVERTING, 扣: Small pieces are arranged in a bowl. A platter is placed on the bowl. Both are turned upside-down. When the bowl is removed, the food will retain the shape of the mold.

MARINATING, 醃 : Mix food with cornstarch, egg yolk or white before cooking. The process "seals" the pieces so that they will be moist inside and crispy outside when Deep-Fried (Sweet and Sour Pork); or velvety when Stir-Fried (Beef and Snow Peas in Oyster Sauce). Besides cornstarch and egg whites, wine, soy sauce and other spices are also used. In the case of Almond Chicken, in which the chicken meat should look white, salt is used instead of soy sauce.

Marinating is also used in Curing and Pickling in which only spices, not cornstarch, are used. Chinese marinade is never full of liquid, Sichuan Pickled Vegetables and Drunken Chicken being the exceptions.

OIL-DRENCHING, 油淋 : Pour boiling oil over already cooked (usually steamed) fish or chicken. The process gives the food a Deep-Fried flavor without actually frying it (Hunan Steamed Fish).

SPLASHING, 烹 : Abruptly pour water, wine and/or seasoning over food toward the end of Stir-Frying (Stir-Fried Carrots) or Shallow-Frying (Splashed Eggs). Because Splashing is done when food is very hot, it absorbs the flavor in a special way which makes the taste quite exciting. You can always splash 1 teaspoon wine toward the end of any Stir-Frying or Shallow-Frying, even though the recipe may not call for it. Try it and taste the difference!

Splashing is also applied to Deep-Fried food. After frying, the food is drained, and heated in a small amount of oil. A sauce is Splashed over the hot food. However, pouring sauce over the food immediately after frying would achieve almost the same effect without using another process and additional oil. Many of my dishes, such as Fried Spring Chicken and Sweet and Sour Fish Slices are prepared this way. The process is referred to as **Velveting** when a thickened sauce is used (See below).

STEEPING, 浸 , is immersing food in boiling liquid very briefly, and turning the heat low, or completely off. The heat retained in the liquid finishes off the cooking. Food cooked this way is tender and juicy, with all the natural flavors preserved.

THICKENING, 勾芡 : Add a paste made of 1 part cornstarch and 2 parts water to make soup or gravy thick. The best way to thicken is to keep the pot boiling at high heat, adding paste and stirring at the same time until the desired consistency is achieved. The amount of cornstarch in the recipe is to be used only as a guide.

VELVETING, 溜 : Pour a sauce thickened with cornstarch over fully cooked food. When the sauce is seasoned with vinegar, it is called **Vinegarine,** 醋溜 . Often sugar is added to the vinegar sauce, creating a sweet and sour dish (Sweet and Sour Pork). Velveting makes food smooth and velvety. The hot gravy tastes very good on steaming hot rice.

MINI RECIPES

BOILED RICE (Reduced Starch): Rinse 1 cup long-grain rice in cold water. Place in pot with 4 cups water. Bring to boil over high heat. Continue boiling over medium heat, uncovered, for 8 minutes. Drain. Cover and cook over low heat for 8 minutes more. Fluff with a fork.

CHILI OIL: You can buy bottled chili oil from the Oriental grocer, but what you make yourself is far superior. You need 1 tablespoon white sesame seeds, 1 cup chili powder, ½ cup vegetable oil, 20 dried chilies (cut into thirds), and 1 teaspoon Sichuan peppercorn.

Toast sesame seeds in a small frying pan until aromatic. Place 1 cup chili powder in a heat-proof bowl. Cover with sesame seeds. Heat oil in wok until very hot. Fry chilies and Sichuan peppercorn. When the chilies turn black, turn heat off. Cool oil to warm (250°F). Remove chilies and peppercorn and discard. Pour oil over the sesame seeds and chili powder. Let cool. Strain and store oil in a cool place in a closed bottle.

CHINESE HOT MUSTARD SAUCE: Place ¼ cup hot mustard powder (such as Colman's Hot Mustard Powder) in a small bowl. Gradually add cold water, stirring as you go, until a smooth paste is formed. Add a few drops of vegetable oil and stir again.

DRIED TANGERINE OR ORANGE PEEL: Wash the fruit. Cut into eighths. Peel (eat the fruit, of course!). Place the peel, white side up, on the cutting board. Scrape off the white pith with a knife until you see the oil sacs in the rind. Let stand at room temperature until dry, about 3 days. Store in a jar at room temperature indefinitely.

EGG FRIED RICE: Heat 2 tablespoons oil in wok until very hot. Add 2 beaten eggs. Stir until set. Add 3 cups cold, cooked rice. Stir. Add ½ teaspoon salt and a pinch of pepper. Drain and chop leftovers. Add to the rice. Exclude any leafy vegetables and soggy items. Throw in frozen peas, bean sprouts, cooked ham, or anything else that suits your fancy. Garnish with chopped scallions.

LEMON DIP: Mix 6 tablespoons sugar, ½ teaspoon salt, 1 teaspoon grated lemon rind, ¼ cup lemon juice, and ¼ cup water. Bring to boil. Thicken with 2 tablespoons cornstarch mixed with 2 tablespoons water. A few drops of yellow food coloring may be added if desired.

NOODLE SOUPS: Bring large pot of water to boil. Boil 1 pound Chinese noodles until cooked, but still firm. Drain and place in tureen. Mix with some oil if not used immediately.

Bring 4 cups broth to boil. Add some stewed meat such as Red-Cooked Pork or Sichuan Beef and some raw leafy vegetables such as spinach or bok choy. When it boils again, pour over noodles. Season with soy sauce and sesame oil.

PLAIN BROTH: Bring a large pot of water to boil. Scald 4 pounds bones (chicken and/or pork) for 1 minute. Drain and rinse under cold water. Bring 4 quarts water to boil, add bones, 3 slices ginger and two whole scallions. Just when it is about to boil again, turn heat low, cover and simmer for 2 hours. You should see only an occasional bubble surfacing. Avoid boiling; it will make the broth cloudy. Drain and strain. Salt to taste. Refrigerate and skim fat. Can be kept in refrigerator for 1 week or frozen for months.

In emergency, use canned chicken broth or bouillon cubes. Dissolve 1 cube in 2 cups of water.

SALT AND PEPPER DIP: Toast equal parts of salt and Sichuan peppercorn in a small frying pan over medium heat for 5 minutes. Shake pan while toasting. When cool, grind in a pepper mill or blend in a blender. Transfer to a small serving plate. The unused portion may be kept in a closed jar.

SCALDED DOUGH: Place 2½ cups all-purpose flour in a mixing bowl. Pour ¾ cup boiling water in, stirring as you go. Add just enough cold water (about ¼ cup) to mop up all the loose flour. Knead on lightly floured board until smooth. Cover with damp cloth and let rest for 30 minutes.

SHRIMP CHIPS: Shrimp chips are fun to serve. Use them in place of potato chips at cocktail parties. You can either buy them already fried or buy the raw chips and fry them yourself. The latter are much better. Make sure that the raw chips are not stale. Fry them in very hot oil (375°F). They should pop up in seconds, otherwise the oil temperature is not hot enough, or the chips are stale. Bake stale chips in oven for 30 minutes. Cool and fry.

SICHUAN PEPPERCORN POWDER: You can buy it in a spice bottle from the Oriental grocer, or you can make it.

Toast ¼ cup Sichuan peppercorn in a small frying pan until aromatic, about 5 minutes. Let cool. Grind in pepper mill or chop in blender. Keep in an airtight jar.

SWEET AND SOUR PINEAPPLE SAUCE: In a blender, blend ½ cup canned pineapple, ½ cup water, 2 tablespoons sugar, 3 tablespoons vinegar, 1 tablespoon dark soy sauce until smooth. Bring to boil. Thicken with 1 tablespoon cornstarch mixed with 2 tablespoons water.

VEGETABLE CARVING: Decorative carvings for garnishes:

Fancy Carrot slices: Trim sides of carrot off to make a square stick. ① Carve out a groove in the center of every side. ② Cut across the stick into thin slices.

Lemon Slice Twist: ③ Slice lemon into very thin slices. ④ Make a slash on one slice from the outside to the center. ⑤ Twist one side of the slice. Orange and limes can also be similarly made into twists.

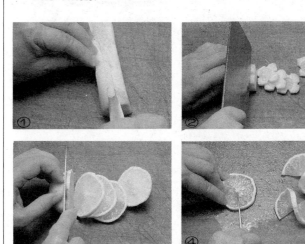

Tomato Crab: Use a firm tomato. ① Slice off the concave side. Set it on the cut-side. ② Make 4 deep vertical slashes, ¼" apart; separate the 5 slices from the rest of the tomato. Deseed. Set on the newly cut surface. ③ Leaving the top slice intact, slash the bottom slices. ④ Spread the bottom slices with fingers.

Scallion Flowers: Use the stem of scallions. Cut off the bulb end. Cut into 2" sections. ⑤ Make a cross on one end, 1" deep. ⑥ Using either knife or scissors, further divide each quarter in half. Soak in iced water until it opens like a flower. To make Scallion Brushes for Peking Duck, cut onion stems into 3" sections and slash both ends.

WINE RICE: You can buy it from the Oriental grocer or make it at home.

You need 2 cups glutinous rice, 1 wine yeast ball, 1 teaspoon all-purpose flour. Rinse rice in cold water. Soak in cold water overnight. Drain. Spread on heat-proof plate and steam for 20 minutes. Rinse in warm water. While rice is still warm, crush the wine yeast ball, mince 1 teaspoon of it fine. Mix with flour. Sprinkle on rice and mix well. Place in a ceramic bowl. Shape a small well in the middle of the rice. Cover with cellophane. Set in a warm place until the well is filled with wine, about 3 days. Refrigerate in a jar. Will keep for months.

YEAST DOUGH: Dissolve 2 tablespoons white sugar in 1 cup very warm, but not hot water (110°F to 115°F). Sprinkle with 1 teaspoon active dry yeast. Cover and leave in a warm place until it bubbles (about 10 minutes).

Place 3 cups all-purpose flour in a bowl, add the yeast mixture gradually, stirring as you go. On a floured board, knead for 5 minutes. (The mixing can also be done in a food processor for 2 minutes. No need to knead.) Add more flour if necessary.

Place dough in a bowl, cover and set in a warm, draft-free place until it doubles in volume, about 2 hours. Now it is ready for use.

For extra light dough, add 1 tablespoon shortening and 1 teaspoon baking powder to the risen dough. Knead and use.

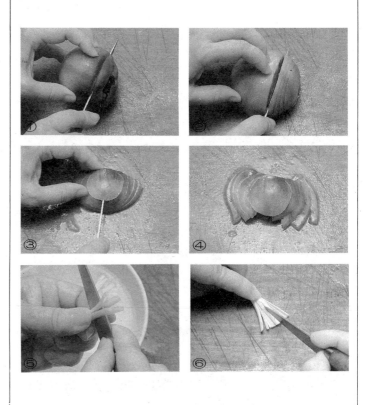

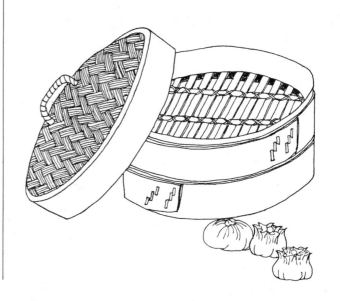

AT THE MARKET

BUYING THE ESSENTIAL EQUIPMENT

You don't need to buy all of Chinatown in order to cook a Chinese meal. You can start right now with just a large iron skillet and a heavy knife. However, I must warn you that Chinese cooking can be highly addictive — you stand in danger of becoming a true *wokaholic!* You will find that you can't help from investing in at least some basic tools to produce culinary feasts for the eye as well as the palate.

CLEAVER ⑤

The cleaver is the most useful and versatile utensil in the kitchen. Once you are familiar with it, you will wonder how you ever got along without it, not only for Chinese cooking, but also for any kind of cooking! If you plan to buy just one thing, be sure to make it the cleaver.

Buy an all-purpose, medium-weight cleaver. The light-weight is for chopping vegetables only, and the heavy-weight is for chopping bones. To identify an all-purpose cleaver, measure the thickest part of the top of the cleaver. It should be around 1/16″ or thicker. Pick it up in your hand and get its feel. Choose the one that you feel most comfortable with.

A carbon-steel cleaver is the most common, and also the most suitable. Stainless steel cleavers are more attractive, but they don't sharpen as well as the carbon steel cleaver.

The disadvantage of a carbon steel cleaver is its tendency to rust. When it is new, scrub it with scouring powder, a steel pad, and hot water to get rid of the protective coating provided by the manufacturer. After each use, wipe it dry and apply a drop of vegetable oil on it to prevent rusting. After it has been used for some time, you do not need to oil it anymore; just keep it dry after each use.

You may either have it professionally sharpened once in a while, or do it yourself by (1) turning a ceramic rice bowl upside down, and *grinding* the blade against the bottom rim of the bowl. Grind in one direction only; not in an up-and-down motion. (2) Turn cleaver and repeat with the other side. (3) You may also use a steel or ceramic sharpener, holding cleaver at an angle, (4) grind the edge across the sharpener. (5) (6) Turn cleaver and repeat with the other side.

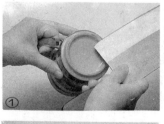

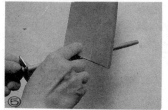

WOK ①

The wok is a marvelous invention. Since it is bowl-shaped, the oil and the food always gravitate toward where the action is, the center, no matter how much food you cook. Therefore, you require less oil than with a flat pan. Food tosses more freely in a wok than in a flat pan, but splatters less. For Deep-Frying, you get a much wider surface area in a wok than in a cylinder-shaped pot with the same amount of oil (see next page).

Buy a 14″ wok, large enough for most jobs, yet small enough to fit most stove tops. It should be made of cast iron or carbon steel, not aluminum, stainless steel, or the non-stick type, because none of them can withstand the intense heat needed for Stir-Frying. An electric wok does not heat and cool down instantaneously; therefore, it is not suitable for Stir-Frying either. But it is a good utensil for Deep-Frying.

Buy one with one wooden handle if you have a strong wrist, otherwise get one with two wooden handles. They will save you from having to reach for the potholders a million times! The wooden-handled wok is rarely found in Chinatown, but is available in department stores.

On an electric stove, use a wok with a flat bottom. I don't recommend using a round-bottomed wok and a collar. Most electric stoves heat slowly. A collar will move the wok away from the source of heat, making it heat even more slowly.

SEASONING THE WOK: A new wok needs to be seasoned. Follow the instructions that come with the wok. If there are none, use the following procedure:

Scrub both the interior and the exterior of the wok with scouring powder, steel pad and hot water to remove the protective coating provided by the manufacturer. Rinse and dry with paper towels. With another paper towel, rub the entire inner surface with vegetable oil, and heat slowly until the oil steams. Remove from the burner and let it cool slightly; wipe clean with a paper towel. Repeat the procedure until the paper towel comes out almost clean.

From now on, do not use scouring powder and steel pad. Use hot water and a nylon pad. Use detergent only if you must. Don't worry about the black coating on your wok; it is your badge of experience; besides, the blacker the wok, the better the cooking.

The following accessories often come with the wok:

②A *spatula* shaped to fit the contour of the wok, very handy for Stir-Frying

③A metal *strainer*, useful for Deep-Frying, Blanching and Plunging

④A pair of frying *chopsticks*

A *tempura rack,* useful for Deep-Frying things such as Spring Rolls

A *rack* useful for Steaming, if you don't have a steamer

⑦A dome-shaped *cover* for Simmering or Smoking

A *collar* to hold the wok securely when you Deep-Fry

If you buy the wok separately, buy a *spatula, a strainer,* and a dome-shaped *cover.* You can always use eating chopsticks for frying

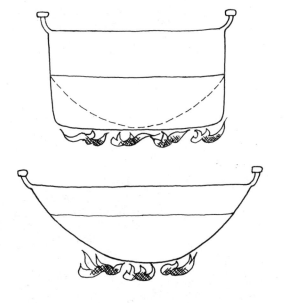

STEAMER

A steamer is very useful for Chinese cooking. Many dishes can be cooked at the same time in one steamer. You can make cakes without an oven. You can keep dishes warm without drying them out.

There are two kinds of steamers on the market. Your choice depends on whether you want beauty or practicality. ⑧ The *bamboo steamer* looks pretty and smells fragrant, but you need to use a wok or a pot larger than the steamer to boil water in. A bamboo steamer comes with two or three tiers and a cover. The size of the bamboo steamers ranges

from a few inches (for a serving of *Dim Sum*) to 3 feet (for restaurants). For home use, it should not be larger than the wok you own. A very small bamboo steamer can also be used as an attractive server.

⑨The practical kind is the *metal steamer.* It consists of four parts: a large pot to boil water in, two perforated tiers to place the food on, and a cover. It is a self-sufficient unit. Buy a 14-inch steamer so that you can steam larger items such as a whole duck.

If you don't want to buy a steamer, use a make-shift one (see p.92).

CHOPSTICKS ④

Chopsticks are used for both cooking and eating. They are extensions of your own fingers. You can pick up small items like ginger root from the hot wok without burning your fingers. You can Deep-Fry with chopsticks, beat eggs with them, and mix batter with them. As for eating, Chinese food simply doesn't taste quite right without chopsticks!

The best kind are the simple bamboo chopsticks. The fancy ones with pointed tips are pretty to look at, but difficult to work with, particularly for beginners.

CLEANING THE CHOPSTICK: To clean chopsticks, rub the whole bunch together between your palms in hot soapy water and rinse. You may also put a bunch of chopsticks in a net (the kind that bean threads are sold in), and put the net in the dishwasher with other utensils.

DISHES

You can serve Chinese dinners using your American dishes. However, it is hard to pick up rice from a plate with chopsticks. Use small dessert bowls for rice; or you can buy rice bowls from Oriental stores. If you also buy china soup spoons, with little saucers for them to rest on, you will be all set to serve any Chinese meal!

OTHER ITEMS

A wooden cutting-board, heavy saucepans, a sand pot ⑩, a heavy iron skillet or a non-stick frying pan, plus a pair of tongs (unless, of course you have mastered the chopsticks) will round out your battery of equipment.

SHOPPING FOR CHINESE INGREDIENTS

Twenty years ago one had to go to Chinatown to buy the ingredients for Chinese cooking. But not any more. Oriental grocery stores are springing up like bamboo shoots after a spring rain. And supermarkets are carrying more and more Chinese ingredients, too. Still, it is worthwhile to go to Chinatown from time to time for better prices and selection, if you live in a metropolitan area.

The following is a list of commonly used Chinese ingredients. The number in the list corresponds to the number in the photographs (p.136, p.140). The "*" symbol indicates the most essential ingredients. For your shopping convinience, take a xerox of the Handy Shopping List (p.148) along to the market.

ABALONE 鮑魚

A delicate-tasting shellfish, used in fancy soups and banquet platters. It is available canned or dried, but occasionally it is available fresh in California. Canned abalone is most often used, Mexican canned abalone being the best. The canned ones are already cooked, so do not overcook. Once the can is opened, leave the abalone in the juice. Keep it in a closed glass jar in the refrigerator for several days or in the freezer for months. The abalone juice is delicious in soups.

AGAR-AGAR 洋菜 ⑦⑥

Processed, dried seaweed made into threads which resemble bean threads. It can be dissolved in boiling water and used in desserts instead of gelatin. It can also be used in salads. First blanch in boiling water; then plunge into cold water to make the salad crunchy. Keep at room temperature indefinitely.

ANISE PEPPERS, see SICHUAN PEPPERCORNS

BABY CORN 玉米筍 ⑨

(Young Corn) Miniature corn, 2 to 3 inches long, available in cans in the States. Used in stir-fried or cold-mixed dishes. Unused portions can be kept in fresh water in a closed jar in the refrigerator for two weeks. Change water twice a week.

BAMBOO SHOOTS 筍 ③

Fibrous shoots from bamboo plants, used in all the 11 methods of Chinese cooking described in this book. The quality depends on the variety of the shoots, as well as the season in which they are harvested. **Winter Bamboo Shoots**(冬筍) small and tender, are considered to be the best tasting. However, they are interchangeable with **Spring Bamboo Shoots**(春筍). Bamboo shoots are sold only in cans in the States, either sliced, shredded or whole; seasoned, or unseasoned. Buy the unseasoned whole ones. Once opened, keep in fresh water for 2 weeks in a closed jar in the refrigerator. Change water twice a week.

BEAD MOLASSES, see SOY SAUCE
BEAN CAKE, see BEAN CURD

BEAN CURD 豆腐

Processed from soy bean milk and pressed into cakes. Used in most of the 11 methods of Chinese cooking described in this book. It is the most important source of protein for Buddhist Vegetarians. It comes in many forms, the most often used varieties being:

Fermented Bean Curd (豆腐乳) Bean curd fermented and preserved in wine and spices. Packaged in glass jars. Comes in white or red color. Used either as a spice or as a relish to accompany rice porridge.

⑧⑤ **Fresh Bean Curd, Bean Curd**(豆腐)Non-porous, custard-like, ivory-colored and bland-tasting. Comes either in 1-lb. plastic box or in blocks immersed in water. The former can be kept in the original package unopened in the refrigerator for one week. The latter can be kept in water in the refrigerator for a few days. Change water daily. Bean curd must be freshly made, should have a fresh soy bean fragrance, and should not smell sour. Freezing will make the taste and texture totally different. Unless you want to use the porous bean curd for soups, don't freeze it. Bean curd comes in either firm or soft form. Most Chinese recipes call for the firm variety.

Instant Soy Bean Curd Can be used when the fresh variety is not available. It can be purchased as powder from Japanese stores. Follow the instructions given on the package, but double the coagulating time to make it firmer. Keep the powder in the refrigerator indefinitely.

⑥⑥ **Pressed Bean Curd** (豆腐干) Fresh Bean Curd with most of the moisture removed by gentle pressure. Comes in 2" squares. If seasoned it looks brown; if unseasoned, it looks ivory. The seasoned type has been simmered in soy sauce, sugar and spices. It is tasty and can be used as a snack by itself, or cold-mixed or stir-fried with other foods. The most flavorful is called **Five-Spiced Pressed Bean Curd** (五香豆腐干). Any seasoned Pressed Bean Curd keeps in the refrigerator for a week in a solution of one tablespoon salt, 2 tablespoons soy sauce, and 4 cups of water. Do not freeze. You can also buy the unseasoned ones and use them in stir-fried or cold-mixed dishes or you can season them by simmering them in spices. Buy Pressed Bean Curd which is fresh-smelling and clear-looking. Reject bean curd which is slimy and which smells sour.

Puffed Bean Curd (油豆腐) Small pieces of bean curd, deep-fried and packaged in plastic bags. Golden-brown outside and porous inside. Can be stuffed with meat and seafood, and then shallow-fried or stewed. Keeps in the refrigerator in plastic bags for two weeks, or frozen for 3 months.

BEAN CURD SKINS, see SOY MILK SKINS
BEAN PASTE, see BEAN SAUCE

BEAN SAUCE 豆瓣醬 ⑥④

A general term for a variety of thick, salty sauces, made from soy beans, sold in cans or jars. The varieties most often used are: **Bean Paste, Brown Bean Paste or Sauce,** or Yellow Bean Sauce (豆瓣醬). Comes either ground (原磨豉) or whole (原晒豉). The ground variety is similar to Japanese miso. It is salty and spicy but not hot.

Hoisin Sauce or Red-Seasoning Sauce, (海鮮醬). A sweet-tasting sauce made of soy beans, sugar, flour, garlic, chili, etc. It is used for seasoning and as a table condiment.

Sichuan Hot Bean Sauce or Chili Paste (辣豆瓣醬) Most essential ingredient in Sichuan cooking. It gives a unique spicy, hot flavor to Sichuan cuisine. Some brands taste hotter than others, so use with caution.

Sweet Bean Paste, Sweet Wheat Sauce, or Peking Sauce (甜麵醬) Similar to Hoisin Sauce, but saltier and less sweet.

Keep all bean sauces in a closed jar in the refrigerator indefinitely.

BEAN SHEETS, see MUNG BEAN SHEETS

BEAN SPROUTS 豆芽

Come in two varieties: **Green Bean Sprouts or Mung Bean Sprouts** (綠豆芽) Small white shoots of mung beans with light green hoods. Used in stir-frying, or blanched and used in salads. Most cookbooks refer to green Bean Sprouts as Bean Sprouts. ㉟

㉞ **Yellow Bean Sprouts or Soy Bean Sprouts** (黃豆芽) Sprouts of soy beans. Larger and coarser than Green Bean Sprouts. Have yellow hoods. They are stir-fried or simmered in soups.

Select sprouts that are crisp with white (not yellow) stems. Keep in the refrigerator immersed in cold water for a week. Change water everyday.

BEAN THREADS 粉絲 ㊼

(Cellophane noodles, peastarch noodles, transparent noodles) Dry noodles made from mung beans. Packaged in bundles of various weights. They are deep-fried, or soaked in warm water and then stir-fried, or used in soups and salads. The 2-oz. bundles are the most convenient. Keep indefinitely at room temperature.

BIRD'S NEST 燕窩

(Swallow's Nest) Lining of swallow's gelatin-like nest made up of tiny fish that they bring home. It is a delicacy used in soups or sweet dishes. Sold in boxes. Must be soaked and cleaned before cooking. The cleaning involves the picking up of tiny feathers, which is most time-consuming. Keep the dried nest at room temperature indefinitely.

BLACK BEANS, see FERMENTED BLACK BEANS

BLACK SESAME SEEDS, see SESAME SEEDS

BOK CHOY, see CABBAGE

BROWN BEAN PASTE, see BEAN SAUCE

CABBAGE 白菜

Of the many varieties grown in China, the following can also be found in the States:

Bok Choy, Chinese Green Cabbage (白菜) White stems with dark green leaves; in some seasons they have yellow flowers.

㉒ **Celery Cabbage** (天津白菜) Sometimes called "Chinese Cabbage" by Americans. The outer leaves are light green, inner ones almost white. The ribs look like celery ribs but the leaves are entirely different from celery leaves.

㉙ **Chinese Broccoli, Gai Lan** (芥蘭) Resembles broccoli in color and taste. However, its stalks are more slender and it does not have florets, as broccoli does. It is more tender than broccoli.

② **Chinese Mustard Greens, Gai Choy** (芥菜) Leaves and stems jade green. Tastes bitter.

⑲ **Napa** (大白菜) Tastes similar to celery cabbage; sweeter and more tender. The plant is shorter and more plump than celery cabbage plant. The outer leaves curl up and wrap the inner leaves.

㉑ **Round Cabbage** (包心白菜) The cabbage that is most familiar to Americans.

All the above varieties can be stir-fried, cooked in soups or pickled. For stir-frying, choose the smaller and tender ones. Although cabbage can be stored in plastic bags in the vegetable compartments of the refrigerator for days, freshly bought ones taste the best.

CELERY CABBAGE, see CABBAGE
CELLOPHANE NOODLES, see BEAN THREADS
CHAR SIU, see CHINESE BARBECUED PORK

CHILI OIL 辣油

(Hot Oil, Hot Pepper Oil) Made by frying chili peppers in oil. Can be either bought from the Oriental grocer or made at home (p.130). It is used in dips and cooking, especially for Sichuan dishes. Keep in a cool place for several months. Some brands are hotter than others; therefore, use with caution.

CHILIES 辣椒 ⑰ (74)

(Chili Peppers) Small pointed hot peppers used in Sichuan dishes. The fresh ones can be either green or red. The dried ones are dark red. They give many Sichuan dishes their spicy taste. Use cautiously because most of them are very hot. Wash hands and cutting board thoroughly after cutting. De-seed and rinse in water if you don't want it too hot. Store dried chilies at room temperature indefinitely; fresh chilies in plastic bags in the refrigerator for weeks.

CHINESE BARBECUED PORK 叉燒

(Char Siu) Cantonese Pork Strips roasted on hooks can be seen hanging behind glass windows in Chinatown. Can be eaten as is, stir-fried with other dishes, or wrapped in *Dim Sum*. It can also be made at home (p.102).

CHINESE BROCCOLI, see CABBAGE

CHINESE CHIVES 韭菜 ㉜

(Garlic Chives) Green grass-like leaves and white stems. They taste like garlic to the Westerner, but not to the Chinese. Used in stir-fried dishes or wrapped in *Dim Sum*. Keep in the refrigerator in plastic bags for a week.

CHINESE CINNAMON 桂皮 (54)

(Cassia Bark) Dried bark of cassia tree. Similar to cinnamon in appearance but more aromatic. Sold either ground or whole. The whole ones are used in stewing and the powder is used as part of *Five-Spiced Powder*. Keep indefinitely in an airtight jar on the shelf.

CHINESE DRIED MUSHROOMS, see MUSHROOMS

CHINESE EGGPLANT 茄子 ㉓

More slender than eggplant. Measures 7 to 9 inches long with purple edible skin and white meat. Can be stewed, stir-fried, or used in cold-mixed dishes. Keep in a plastic bag in the vegetable box in the refrigerator for up to two weeks.

CHINESE GREEN CABBAGE, see CABBAGE

CHINESE MUSTARD GREENS, see CABBAGE

CHINESE NOODLES 蛋麵 ㊴

(Egg Noodles) Made of eggs and wheat flour. They are boiled first; then cooked with meats and vegetables. Available fresh or dried. The fresh ones can be kept in the refrigerator for two weeks; or in the freezer, tightly wrapped, for months. Frozen noodles should be dropped in boiling water while still frozen. Keep the dried noodles on shelf indefinitely.

CHINESE PARSLEY, see FRESH CORIANDER

CHINESE PEA PODS, see SNOW PEAS

CHINESE SAUSAGE 香腸 ㊾

Comes in two varieties:

Meat Sausage is chopped, marinated pork stuffed in intestines and cured. It is reddish-looking and sweet-tasting. Can be either steamed, sliced and eaten as is, or diced and used in stuffing.

Liver Sausage is chopped, marinated liver stuffed in the intestines and cured. Dark and tasty. Used as a side dish or appetizer after being steamed and sliced.

Chinese Sausages can be placed in a plastic bag and kept in the refrigerator for months.

CHINESE TURNIPS, see ICICLE RADISH

CHINESE VINEGAR 醋

Comes in a variety of colors and flavors. The most commonly used variety in Chinese cooking is **Rice Vineger** (米醋) which tastes mild and looks pale. It is now available in supermarkets. Use it whenever vinegar is called for. Substitute white wine vinegar for Rice Vinegar; but use less.

CHINESE WINE 酒 (81)

***Cooking Wines: Rice Wine** (米酒) is most commonly used. Low in alcoholic content. Unlike French cooking, in which you taste the wine, in Chinese cooking you do not taste the wine. Therefore, whenever wine is called for, use any dry wine or sherry that is too stale to drink. Only "Drunken Dishes" such as Drunken Chicken have a strong wine taste; use *Shaohsing Wine*.

CHRYSANTHEMUMS 菊花 ⑦⑨

The fresh large white chrysanthemums are used for fire pots. Buy them from the florist or pick them from your garden. The tiny, daisy-like little blossoms which are dried come in plastic bags, and are used to make Chrysanthemum Tea.

CILANTRO, see FRESH CORIANDER
CLOUD EARS, see MUSHROOMS
DARK SOY SAUCE, see SOY SAUCE
DIACONE, see ICICLE RADISH
DOUFU, see BEAN CURD

DOUSHA 豆沙 ⑦①

(Red Bean Paste) A thick, sweetened paste made from red beans. Sold in cans, used for sweet dishes. Should not be confused with *Sweet Wheat Sauce*, which is a savory paste, sweet and salty. Keeps indefinitely in a jar in the refrigerator.

DRAGON'S EYES 龍眼·桂圓 ⑥①

(Logans) Round, marble-sized fruit, with smooth, brown skin. The thin pulp wraps around the black, shiny pits which resemble the dragon's eyes. The dried meat is sold in packages, tastes like raisins and is used to make sweet dishes. Keeps in a closed jar on the shelf indefinitely.

DRIED JELLYFISH 海蜇皮 ④⑦

Yellowish brown and opaque sheets folded and wrapped in plastic paper. They are soaked, cleaned and shredded and used in salads. Dry jellyfish keeps on the shelf indefinitely.

DRIED LOTUS SEEDS, see LOTUS SEEDS

DRIED MUSHROOMS, see MUSHROOMS

DRIED SCALLOPS 干貝 ⑥⑦

Look like scallops, but darker and rock-hard. Although they are expensive, a little bit goes a long way. They add delicious flavor to soups and vegetables. Do not substitute fresh scallops for dried scallops. Keep indefinitely on the shelf.

DRIED SHRIMP 蝦米 ㊻

Pinkish and salty. Packaged in plastic bags. Do not let the pungent smell discourage you. Once soaked and cooked with meat or vegetables, it makes everything delicious. Don't over-soak. Don't substitute fresh shrimp for dried. Keep in an airtight jar on the shelf indefinitely (away from gourmet cats).

DRIED TANGERINE PEEL 陳皮

Sold in plastic bags as a spice. Used in stewed dishes, such as duck or *lu* beef. It can also be made at home (see p. 130). Keeps in a closed jar on the shelf indefinitely.

DRIED TIGER LILIES 金針 ㊺

(**Tiger Lily Buds, Golden Needles**) Dried buds, brown in color, about 3 inches long. They are soaked in warm water for 15 minutes and cooked with meats and other vegetables. Dried buds will keep for months at room temperature. To inhibit insect growth in warm climate, place buds in the freezer for 48 hours in the spring.

DUCK SAUCE, see PLUM SAUCE

EGG NOODLES, see CHINESE NOODLES

EGG ROLL SKINS or WRAPPERS 春捲皮 ⑦⑦

Made of flour, water, and a very small amount of egg. Wrapped in 6-inch square packages and kept in the refrigerator or freezer at the store. They are used to make egg rolls in Chinese restaurants. Can be wrapped and kept in the refrigerator for two weeks, and in the freezer for 3 months. Wrap the frozen skin in damp cloth when thawing. See **Spring Roll Skins.**

FERMENTED BEAN CURD, see BEAN CURD

FERMENTED BLACK BEANS 豆豉 ⑥②

(**Black Beans**) Small black beans, fermented and preserved in ginger and salt. Sold in plastic bags. Used as a spice. Can be kept on the shelf indefinitely. Do not be concerned if white powder appears on the beans; it is only the salt.

FISH BALLS 魚球 ㊷

White, smooth balls made of fish, egg whites, and cornstarch. Used in soups and stews. They are kept in bags in freezers at the Oriental stores. Keep frozen until ready to use.

FIVE-SPICE POWDER 五香粉

A strong, aromatic combination of ground star anise, fennel, cloves, Chinese cinnamon, and Sichuan Peppercorn. The aroma can be overwhelming; therefore, use sparingly. Keep in an airtight jar indefinitely.

FIVE-SPICE RICE FLOUR 五香米粉

(**Steam Powder, Spicy Rice Mixture**) Coarsely-ground rice flour mixed with spices, used to coat meat for steamed dishes. Keep in an airtight jar in a dry place indefinitely.

FRESH CORIANDER 香菜,芫荽 �37

(**Chinese Parsley, Cilantro**) Looks somewhat like parsley. Has a strong, unique aroma. A person can either love it or hate it. But, of course, you can learn to like it. It has a marvelous aroma when used as a garnish or seasoning. Keep the root-end in water in a glass jar and cover the top with a plastic bag, tied to the jar with a rubber band, and place the jar in the refrigerator. The leaves will be kept green for 2 to 3 weeks. Substitute whole scallions or parsley for fresh coriander.

FRESH EGG NOODLES, see CHINESE NOODLES

FRESH GINGER, see GINGER

*GINGER 薑 ㉝

(**Ginger Root**) Knobby, aromatic, spicy plant. Looks like Jerusalem artichokes. Does wonders to food, particularly to poultry and sea food. Most ginger is **Mature Ginger** (老薑) and is used as a spice. Select ginger which is large and firm with smooth skin. Buy in small quantities. Keep in plastic bag in the vegetable box of the refrigerator for weeks. If mold appears, scrape it off, and use the rest. Ginger may be kept immersed in dry wine indefinitely in a closed jar in the refrigerator. Ginger usually does not have to be peeled, particularly when it is going to be discarded later. Dry ginger is not a good substitute. If you must use it, use only half the required quantity. Occasionally, **Young Ginger** (嫩薑) is available in the market. It is more tender and less spicy. It can be used as a vegetable.

GAI CHOY, see CABBAGE
GAI LAN, see CABBAGE
GOLDEN NEEDLE MUSHROOMS,
see MUSHROOMS
GOLDEN NEEDLES,
see DRIED TIGER LILIES
GLUTEN PUFF, see MOCK MEAT
GLUTINOUS RICE, see RICE
GLUTINOUS RICE FLOUR,
see RICE FLOUR
GREEN BEAN SPROUTS,
see BEAN SPROUTS

HAM 火腿 ㊽

Yunan Ham from China is difficult to find in the States. **Smithfield Ham** is closest to Yunan Ham in taste and texture. Ham is used as a main dish and also as a spice or garnish. You can buy cooked Smithfield ham from gourmet shops or raw ham from Chinese grocery shops. When used as a spice, buy only small quantities. Cooked ham can be kept in the refrigerator for 2 months, uncooked ham indefinitely. Other hams, such as Westphalian are also good substitutes for Chinese ham. The soft, less spicy boiled ham sold in supermarkets cannot be used as a spice in Chinese cooking.

HEAVY SOY SAUCE, see SOY SAUCE
HOISIN SAUCE, see BEAN SAUCE
HOT PEPPER OIL, see Chili Oil

ICICLE RADISH 蘿蔔 ⑤

(**Chinese Radish, Chinese Turnip, Loboh** in **Chinese** and **Daicone** in **Japanese**) Tastes like white radish. Larger ones can be over 18 inches long. Can be stir-fried, stewed, or made into salads and pickles. Select the ones which are firm and solid. Keep in the vegetable box in the refrigerator for weeks.

INSTANT BEAN CURD, see BEAN CURD

JAHTSAI 榨菜 ㊾

(**Sichuan Preserved Vegetables, Sichuan Preserved Kahlrabi**) Twisted, olive-colored vegetables preserved in a reddish chili paste. Used as a spice. Sold in cans or by the pound. Store in a glass jar in the refrigerator indefinitely. Rinse in cold water before using unless you like it very hot.

JASMINE TEA, see p.155
JELLYFISH, see DRIED JELLYFISH

JIAOTZE SKINS 餃子皮

Round discs about 4 inches in diameter, made of flour and water. Used to wrap *Jiaotze* or *Guotieh*. Store in the refrigerator for 2 weeks or in the freezer for 3 months. When thawing, wrap in damp cloth.

JUJUBE 棗 ㊷

Dried fruit with puckered skin. Used in sweet dishes and in stuffing. They can be either red (**Red Date**, 紅棗), or black (**Black Date**, 黑棗). Dried jujube will keep at room temperature indefinitely.

KUMQUAT 金桔

A small, oval, orange-colored citrus fruit, sold either fresh, dried, or canned. Can be eaten as fruit or cooked in sweet dishes.

LARGE BEAN CURD SKIN,
see SOY MILK SKIN

LAVER 紫菜

Purple, paper-thin seaweed used in soups. Keep at room temperature indefinitely.

LICHEE 荔枝

(**Lichee Nuts**) A fruit with reddish bumpy skin and opaque meat, sold dried or canned, or occasionally fresh. Can be eaten as fruit or used in desserts or sweet and sour dishes.

LIGHT SOY SAUCE, see SOY SAUCE
LONG GRAIN RICE, see RICE
LONGANS, see DRAGON'S EYES

LOQUAT 枇杷

Small, teardrop-shaped fruit with light yellow skin and delicate-tasting pulp. Sold in cans in the States. Can be eaten as fruit or made into desserts.

LOTUS ROOTS 藕 ④

Root of lotus plant, shaped like two or three tubes of salami linked together. The cross section looks like a cartwheel. It can be stewed, stir-fried or cold-mixed. It is sold fresh, canned, or dried. The dried one is already sliced, tastes different from the fresh root, must be soaked before cooking.

LOTUS SEEDS 蓮子 ㊸

Brown, marble-sized seeds of lotus plants. These exotic seeds are used in soups, sweet dishes or stuffing. They come either canned or dried. Dried seeds must be soaked before cooking. Keep dried seeds at room temperature indefinitely.

MOCK ABALONE, see MOCK MEAT

MOCK CURRIED CHICKEN, see MOCK MEAT

MOCK MEAT 齋肉 ㊶

Vegetarian food made of soy beans or **Wheat Gluten** (麵筋) which is also called **Puffed Wheat.** The food resembles non-vegetarian food in taste and texture. You can order virtually any dish that looks and tastes like any animal product from a vegetarian restaurant. Several are manufactured and canned, such as **Mock Abalone,** 齋鮑魚 ,**Mock Curried Chicken,** 咖哩齋雞肉, etc.

MONOSODIUM GLUTAMATE 味精

(m.s.g.) A crystalline extract from soy beans used to enhance the flavor of food. I rarely use m.s.g. in my cooking, not only because some people are allergic to it, but also because good food is made of good quality material and good workmanship, not artificial flavoring. However, certain foods, such as *Wontons,* are traditionally seasoned with m.s.g. and a dash of it does make the difference in taste. Experiment with it, if you are not allergic to it.

MUNG BEAN SHEETS 粉皮 (51)

Made from mung beans by the same process as Bean Threads, except that bean sheets are made into sheets and packed in plastic bags. They can be soaked and used in salads. Keep dried bean sheets at room temperature indefinitely.

MUNG BEAN SPROUTS, see BEAN SPROUTS

MUSHROOMS 菇

In addition to the mushrooms listed below, fresh mushrooms from supermarkets are also used in Chinese cooking.

Button Mushrooms, Similar to *champignons* in size and flavor. Sold in cans.

㊳ **Golden Needle Mushroom** (金針菇) Looks almost like bean sprouts. Sold canned or occasionally fresh.

㉗ **Straw Mushrooms** (草菇) Umbrella-shaped mushrooms with a slippery texture and mild taste. Grown on straw. Available in cans.

(80) ***Winter Mushrooms, Dried Mushrooms, Dried Black Mushrooms** (冬菇) Used in all the 11 cooking methods described in this book. The better quality mushrooms are larger and plumper. The top of the cup is dark brown and the bottom and stem are beige. They are soaked in warm water for 20 minutes before cooking, but soaking overnight in cold water will make them more succulent. Their flavor is unique and fresh mushrooms are not to be used as substitutes.

㊹ **Wood Ears, Tree Ears** (木耳) Called **Cloud Ears** (雲耳) by the Cantonese, they are dark fungus grown on wood. The smallest variety are a half-inch wide and are shaped like the ears of a little mouse. The large ones can be as large as 3 inches wide. They can be used in soups or stir-fried dishes. They don't have much flavor of their own, but they do have an interesting texture.

Dried mushrooms will keep at room temperature indefinitely. The canned ones will keep in a closed jar in the refrigerator for a week.

NAPA, see CABBAGE
NOODLES, see CHINESE NOODLES
OOLONG TEA, see p.155
ORIENTAL SESAME SEED OIL, see SESAME OIL

OYSTER SAUCE 蠔油

Thick brown sauce made from oyster extract, salt, soy sauce, and spices. Adds marvelous flavor to eggs, beef, poultry, and cold-mixed dishes. Keeps well at room temperature, but longer in the refrigerator.

PEASTARCH NOODLES, see BEAN THREAD

PEKING SAUCE, see BEAN SAUCE

PLUM SAUCE 梅蘇醬

(Duck Sauce) A sweet, spicy sauce made from plums. Sold in jars or cans. Many Chinese-American restaurants use it as a table condiment. Keeps in a jar in the refrigerator indefinitely.

PRESERVED DUCK EGGS 皮蛋 ⑦⓪

(Thousand-Year-Old Eggs) Duck eggs preserved in ashes, lime, rice husks and clay not quite for a thousand years, nor even one hundred years, nor even one year, but just 3 months. The egg white is amber and the yolk is dark green. Sprinkled with soy sauce and sesame oil, the eggs taste delicious to the Chinese. Keep at room temperature indefinitely.

PRESSED BEAN CURD, see BEAN CURD
PUFFED BEAN CURD, see BEAN CURD
RED BEAN PASTE, see DOUSHA
RED DATES, see JUJUBE

RICE 米

The two major varieties are:

*Regular Rice (米) Comes in long grain and short grain. The former makes fluffy rice and is used by Chinese restaurants. The latter is stickier and is widely used in Taiwan and Japan. Regular rice keeps for months on the shelf.

⑥③ Glutinous Rice or Sweet Rice (糯米) Also comes in long grain and short grain. Only the short grain is sold in the States. Both varieties are used in sweet dishes or as stuffing. Since glutinous rice can become rancid easily, it is best to keep it in the refrigerator.

RICE FLOUR

Rice flour comes in the following forms:

Glutinous Rice Flour (糯米粉) Used to make *Dim Sum*. Can be kept in the refrigerator indefinitely.

Regular Rice Flour (粘米粉) Used to make *Dim Sum*. Can be kept at room temperature.

Steam Powder or Spicy Rice Mixture (五香米粉) A coarse-ground rice powder mixed with spices, used to coat meat or poultry for steaming. Can be kept in an airtight jar at room temperature indefinitely.

RICE NOODLES, see RICE STICKS
RICE POWDER, see RICE FLOUR

RICE STICKS 米粉 ⑧③

(Rice Noodles) Long, brittle noodles, made of regular rice flour. They are soaked first, and then stir-fried, or cooked in soups. The Chinese restaurants deep-fry them to make them into garnish. Keep at room temperature indefinitely.

RICE VINEGAR, see CHINESE VINEGAR
RICE WINE PASTE, see WINE RICE

ROCK CANDY 冰糖 ⑥⑤

(Rock Sugar) Crystallized sugar, amber in color and irregular in shape. Used in stewed dishes to enhance the flavor and add a glaze. Keep at room temperature indefinitely.

ROCK SUGAR, see ROCK CANDY

SALTED BLACK BEANS, see FERMENTED BLACK BEANS

SATAY SAUCE 沙爹醬

A hot, spicy sauce made of ground peanuts, coconut milk, chilies, onions and salt. It originated in Malaysia, and is now widely used in Taiwan as a table condiment with Fire Pot.

SEA CUCUMBER 海參 ⑥⑧

(Beche-de-Mer) A primitive sea animal in the shape and size of a cucumber. Dark brown in color. It is used in exotic soups and stews. Requires an acquired taste to appreciate its gelatin-like texture, and almost tasteless taste. Only available dried in the States. It is time-consuming to prepare sea cucumbers. Keep the dried ones at room temperature indefinitely.

SECOND LAYER BEAN CURD, see SOY MILK SKIN

*SESAME OIL 麻油

(Sesame Seed Oil, Oriental Sesame Seed Oil) Extract from roasted sesame seeds, aromatic and darker than salad oil. It is used as garnish or as a table condiment, not for stir-frying or deep-frying. Do not confuse it with the odorless variety made of unroasted seeds sold in health food stores. Sesame oil keeps for 3 months at room temperature, indefinitely in the refrigerator. The cold oil looks cloudy in the refrigerator, but shaking it at room temperature will restore its original color.

SESAME SEED PASTE 芝麻醬

A paste made from ground, roasted sesame seeds, resembles peanut butter in color and texture. Has a distinct sesame fragrance. It should be gradually mixed with water or broth until a smooth paste is formed before being used in salads or as a table condiment. You can substitute peanut butter for sesame seed paste, but you need to add a few drops of sesame oil to get the sesame flavor. *Tahini*, a mid-eastern paste made of unroasted sesame seeds is *not* a suitable substitute. Keep sesame seed paste in a jar in a cool place indefinitely.

SESAME SEEDS 芝麻 (59)

Tiny seeds which can be either black or white. When toasted, they are very aromatic. They are used in *Dim Sum*, or as a garnish. Keep well at room temperature, but even better in the refrigerator.

SHANGHAI SPRING ROLL WRAPPERS, see SPRING ROLL SKINS

SHAOHSING WINE, see CHINESE WINE

SHARK'S FIN 魚翅

Cartilage from shark's fin. A delicacy used for banquets. It is sold either dried or canned. It is time-consuming to process the dried fin. It keeps at room temperature indefinitely.

SHRIMP CHIPS 蝦片

Either white or pastel-colored chips, made of shrimp and starch. They are sold in boxes. They puff up in hot oil and are used as appetizers or as a garnish. Can be stored for several days in a cool, dry place. Since moisture will prevent proper frying of the chips, stale chips must be baked in an oven for 30 minutes, and cooled before frying.

SICHUAN HOT BEAN SAUCE, see BEAN SAUCE

SICHUAN PEPPERCORNS 花椒 (55)

(Flower Peppers, Anise Peppers) Reddish brown peppercorns which are not as smooth as peppercorns. They taste milder than most peppers, but produce a numbing sensation. They are usually sold whole. Grind them in a pepper mill or a blender; or crush them with the handle of a cleaver (see p. 13). Use the powder for stir-fried and cold-mixed dishes. Use whole corns for curing and stewing. Store indefinitely in an airtight jar at room temperature.

SICHUAN PRESERVED KOHLRABI, see JAHTSAI

SICHUAN PRESERVED VEGETABLES, see JAHTSAI

SNOW PEAS 雪豆 ⑱

(Chinese Pea Pods) Small green peas with flat edible pods. Sweet and crunchy, delicious in stir-fried dishes. They must be stringed before cooking. Select thin, tender, crisp pods. Avoid using frozen snow peas which are soggy. If fresh ones are unavailable, use peeled and sliced broccoli stems instead.

SOY MILK SKIN 豆腐皮 (75)

(Bean Curd Skin) Solidified surface formed by boiling soy milk. The top surface is lifted and dried. The thicker kind are called **the second layer,** 二竹片. They are cut into rectangular pieces and packaged in 1/2-lb. size. The thinner kind are called **Bean Curd Sheet, or Large Bean Curd Skin;** 腐竹皮. Either rectangular or half-moon-shaped, they are paper-thin and are used as wrappers for deep-frying. They are fragile. Broken pieces can be mended with moistened scraps. The thicker variety keep at room temperature for 3 months, while the thinner kind keep in the refrigerator for several days.

SOUR PLUM 酸梅

Plum preserved in salt. Can be used as a snack (very salty and sour), or added to make wine taste fruity.

SOY SAUCE 醬油

Made from fermented soy beans, flour and salt. The most common varieties are:

*Dark Soy Sauce, Heavy Soy Sauce (老抽) Thicker than the light soy sauce and fermented for a longer period. Molasses is added. The sauce is indispensable for stewing.

*Light Soy Sauce, Thin Soy Sauce (生抽) Used in fish, white chicken meat, and any other food whose light color you want to preserve. It is also used as a table condiment. *Kikkoman Soy Sauce,* a popular Japanese brand, can be used as a light soy sauce. Unless specified, use either dark or light soy sauce.

A much less frequently used variety *is **Thick Soy Sauce or Bead Molasses** (珠油)* A thick, almost black sauce used for some cold-mixed dishes to make them taste and look rich. Many Chinese-American restaurants use it to darken fried rice.

All varieties of soy sauce keep indefinitely at room temperature.

SPRING ROLL SKINS or WRAPPERS 上海春捲皮 ⑦

(Shanghai Spring Roll Wrappers) Thin crepes, hand-made individually. Used to wrap spring rolls and other food. Tightly-wrapped skins will keep in the refrigerator for a week, or in the freezer for a month. When thawing, wrap them in damp cloth. Dried-out skins can sometimes be restored by wrapping in a damp cloth also.

STAR ANISE 八角 ㊶

Star-shaped, and wooden-textured brown seed pod with a strong licorice aroma. Sold in plastic bags. Provide wonderful aroma to stewed dishes. Use this powerful spice only sparingly. Keeps in an airtight jar at room temperature indefinitely.

STEAM POWDER, see RICE FLOUR
STICKY RICE, see RICE
STRAW MUSHROOMS,
see MUSHROOMS
SWEET WHEAT SAUCE,

see BEAN SAUCE
SWEET RICE, see RICE
TEA, see p.155
THIN SOY SAUCE, see SOY SAUCE

TIENTSIN PRESERVED VEGETABLE 天津冬菜 ㊲

Celery cabbage preserved with salt, garlic and other spices, sold in ceramic urns. Used in stewed dishes such as red-cooked duck, or stir-fried with other vegetables. Keeps in the original container at room temperature indefinitely.

TIGER LILY BUDS,
see DRIED TIGER LILIES
TOFU, see BEAN CURD
TRANSPARENT NOODLES,
see BEAN THREADS
TREE EARS, see MUSHROOMS
VEGETABLE STEAK, see MOCK MEAT
VINEGAR, see CHINESE VINEGAR

WATER CHESTNUTS 荸薺 ㊵

Not nuts, but bulbs of an aquatic plant. About the size of a walnut, with brown skin and white meat. Add sweetness and crunchiness to many a dish. Mostly sold in cans, already peeled. Store unused portion in a jar in the refrigerator. Change the water twice a week. Will keep for 3 weeks. Occasionally fresh ones are available. They are even sweeter and crunchier than the canned ones. Keep unpeeled fresh water chestnuts in the refrigerator for weeks, or in the freezer for months.

WHEAT GLUTEN, see MOCK MEAT
WHITE SESAME SEEDS, see
SESAME SEEDS
WINE, see CHINESE WINE

WINE RICE 酒釀 ㊿

(Wine Sauce) Fermented glutinous rice, sold in jars together with its residue. Used in sauces and sweet dishes. Store in its original container in the refrigerator for weeks.

WINE SAUCE, see WINE RICE

WINTER MELON 冬瓜 ㉘

A melon-sized squash with tough, green skin and soft, white meat. Delicate-tasting, used in soups and stews. Sold by the pound, either whole or in slices. Once opened, the winter melon can be kept in a plastic bag in the refrigerator for a week.

WINTER MUSHROOMS, see MUSHROOMS

WONTON SKINS or WRAPPERS 餛飩皮 ⑧²

Three-and-a-half inch square skins made of flour, water and eggs, wrapped in 1 lb. packages, with 65-150 pieces each. Buy the thin variety. If not available, quarter thin egg roll skins into wonton wrappers. Wrap tightly and store in the refrigerator for two weeks or in the freezer for three months. When thawing, wrap the skins in a damp cloth.

WOOD EARS, see MUSHROOMS
YELLOW BEAN SPROUTS, see BEAN SPROUTS
YOUNG GINGER, see GINGER
YUAN MO SHIH, see BEAN SAUCE
YUAN SHAI SHIH, see BEAN SAUCE
YUNAN HAM, see HAM

HANDY SHOPPING LIST

CANNED GOODS
Abalone 鮑魚
Baby Corn 玉米筍
Bamboo Shoots 筍
Dousha 豆沙
Golden Needle Mushrooms 金針菇
Jahtsai 榨菜
Lichee 荔枝
Loquat 枇杷
Mock Meat 齋鮑魚・咖哩齋雞肉
Tientsin Preserved Vegetables 天津冬菜
Water Chestnuts 荸薺

OILS, SAUCE, ETC.
Chili Oil 辣油
Chinese Vinegar 醋
Hoisin Sauce 海鮮醬
Oyster Sauce 蠔油
Plum Sauce 梅蘇醬
Satay Sauce 沙爹醬
Sesame Oil 麻油
Sesame Seed Paste 芝蔴醬
Sichuan Hot Bean Sauce 辣豆瓣醬
Soy Sauce, Dark 老抽
Soy Sauce, Light 生抽
Wine Rice 酒釀
Yellow Bean Sauce 豆瓣醬

FRESH VEGETABLES
Bean Sprouts 豆芽
Bok Choy 白菜
Chili 辣椒
Chinese Broccoli 芥蘭
Chinese Chives 蓮菜
Chinese Eggplant 茄子
Chinese Mustard Green 芥菜
Coriander, Fresh 芫荽
Ginger 薑
Icicle Radishes 蘿蔔
Lotus Roots 藕
Snow Peas 雪豆
Water Chestnuts 荸薺
Winter Melon 冬瓜

REFRIGERATOR ITEMS
Bean Curd, Fresh 豆腐
Bean Curd, Pressed 豆腐干
Egg Noodles 蛋麵
Eggroll Skins 春捲皮
Jiaotze Skins 餃子皮
Spring Roll Skins 上海春捲皮
Wonton Skins 餛飩皮

OTHER ITEMS
Cantonese Roast Duck 燒鴨
Chinese Barbecued Pork 叉燒

DRIED GOODS
Agar-Agar 洋菜
Bean Threads 粉絲
Chinese Cinnamon 桂皮
Chinese Ham 火腿
Chinese Sausage 香腸
Chrysanthemums 菊花
Dragon's Eyes 龍眼・桂圓
Dried Jelly Fish 海蜇皮
Dried Mushrooms 冬菇
Dried Scallops 干貝
Dried Shrimp 蝦米
Dried Tangerine Peel 陳皮
Dried Tiger Lilies 金針
Fermented Black Beans 豆豉
Five-Spice Powder 五香粉
Five-Spice Rice Powder 五香米粉
Jujube 紅棗
Kumquat 金桔
Laver 紫菜
Lichee 荔枝
Loquat 枇杷
Lotus Roots 藕
Lotus Seeds 蓮子
Preserved Duck Eggs 皮蛋
Rice, Glutinous 糯米
Rice, Regular 米
Rice Flour, Glutinous 糯米粉
Rice Flour, Regular 粘米粉
Rice Sticks 米粉
Rock Candy 冰糖
Sea Cucumbers 海參
Soy Milk Skin 豆腐皮
Sesame Seeds 芝蔴
Shark's Fin 魚翅
Shrimp Chips 蝦片
Sichuan Peppercorn 花椒
Sour Plums 酸梅
Star Anise 八角
Tapioca Powder 太白粉
Tea 茶
Wood Ears 木耳

AT HOME

MENU PLANNING

Where there is no planning, parties perish.

START SIMPLY

Start your menu with one or two dishes that are easy to make, and can be prepared ahead of time. Make judicious additions to that base and build up something more elaborate.

Keep two principles in mind:

1. Use a variety of MATERIALS to achieve contrasts in color and shape, texture and taste.

2. Use a variety of METHODS to avoid last-minute rush.

SERVING SIZE

Except for one-dish meals, it is pointless to designate the serving size for dishes, because how many people a dish serves depends on how many other dishes are served.

Use proportionally more food for company than for family meals.

To estimate if you have enough food for your guests, use the following guide.

Meat:

½ pound meat without bones per person or

1 pound seafood per person or

1 pound poultry with bones per person

Add the weight of all meat, poultry, seafood, etc. in your recipes together for a ball-park figure.

Vegetables:

1 vegetable dish and 2 non-vegetable dishes to serve Americans

2 or more vegetable dishes and 3 non-vegetable dishes to serve Chinese

BEVERAGES:

The Chinese offer tea as the guests arrive. Tea cups are withdrawn when dinner starts.

The only liquid at family meals is soup. At dinner parties, ladies drink soda or fruity wines, while men drink anything from soda or beer to hard liquor.

APPETIZERS:

Shrimp chips are the easiest. Various smoked items and cured items, as well as savory *Dim Sum*, can be used as appetizers.

RICE:

Plain rice is served with most meals but not at banquets. The plainness of the rice brings out the character of each dish, as a simple frame provides the setting for a stunning picture. The Northerners eat Steamed Buns with meals, or wrap various items in Thin Cakes.

WORKING PERSON'S MENU

During the weekend, prepare several dishes using the following:

Easy Methods: The following methods are not only easy to apply, but also can be used to make larger quantities:
Stewing
Steaming
Baking
Curing
Pickling
Cold-Mixing

Freeze them in portions to suit your needs (¼ to ⅓ recipe per person). In the morning when you leave for work, you can transfer a portion from the freezer to the refrigerator. When you come back in the evening, it will be thawed enough for you to dress it up in different ways. For instance, serve Sweet and Sour Spareribs over spinach one day and with a cold-mixed vegetables another day.

Stir-Fried Food: If you like stir-fried food, you can cut up large quantities of meat or chicken over the weekend and marinate. Make small packages of suitable portions (¼ to ⅓ recipe per person), and put them in empty orange juice cans to freeze. Transfer to the refrigerator in the morning and stir-fry in the evening.

One-Dish Meals: There are several one-dish meals that can be easily made by the working person:

Jiaotze: Simply make during the weekend and freeze. Re-heat in the steamer or microwave oven.

Wonton Soup: When you feel really ambitious, wrap a lot of *wontons* and put them in the freezer between wax paper sprinkled with flour. You can take a shortcut as a working person, and heat a can of chicken broth. Drop the frozen *wontons* in boiling water and boil for 5 minutes and drain. Combine with boiling broth, and some spinach, and you have Wonton Soup!

Egg Fried Rice: Use leftover food or ready-made food such as Barbecued Pork.

Beef Noodle Soup: Boil noodles. Re-heat any kind of stewed beef and pour over. Add broth if necessary.

One-Dish Meals served with Boiled Rice or Steamed Buns
Lion's Head Casserole
Red-Cooked Pork with Vegetables
Almond Chicken
Beef and Snowpeas in Oyster Sauce
Pork and Peppers

Two-Dish Meals Served with Boiled Rice or Steamed Buns
Shallow-Fried Fish
Stir-Fried String Beans

Yellow-Smothered Chicken
Sichuan Pickled Vegetables

Spinach Soup
Bean Sauce Pork

Sweet and Sour Spareribs
Stir-Fried Cabbage

COOK-INS

At a Cook-In, your guests not only eat with you, but they also cook with you.

1. Guests come in casual clothes and bring their own aprons, cutting boards and cleavers.

2. Hostess prepares all the materials and recipes.

3. Guests choose one particular dish to cook.

4. Hostess assigns the cooking order of the dishes.

5. Guests set the table at the hostess' direction.

6. Ask the guests to say something particular that they like about each dish. This adds to the enjoyment of the dinner!

SNACK PARTIES

Instead of a complete dinner, you may want to have one of the following Snack Parties:
Jiaotze Party
Wonton Party
Dim Sum Party, including Thin Cakes, Mushu Pork, Pork Shreds in Peking Sauce, etc. You can also convert any Snack Party into a Cook-In.

BUFFETS

Chinese-style buffets are popular in China and

overseas. Only a few eating utensils are needed: plates and chopsticks; soups bowls and soup spoons (if a soup is served).

Choose one or two from the following groups:

Cold Dishes
　　Curing
　　Pickling
　　Cold-Mixing
　　Stewed dishes, such as Lu Beef, Tea Eggs, Sichuan Peppercorn Chicken

Dishes that can be kept warm in steamer or on hottray, or re-heated in microwave oven
　　Pearl Balls
　　Silver Thread Rolls
　　Shrimp Custard
　　Steamed Beef Bowls

Dishes that can be kept warm on hottray or warm oven or re-heated in microwave oven
　　Shallow-Fried Fish Slices
　　Sweet and Sour Spareribs
　　Stuffed Mushrooms
　　Baked Pork Rolls
　　Lion's Head Casserole
　　Sichuan Beef
　　Curried Chicken

Dishes that can be re-heated in a 350°F. oven, but preferably refried:
　　Spring Rolls (any kind)
　　Shrimp Balls (any kind)
　　Shrimp Toast
　　Fried Wontons

Soups that retain their attractive appearance
　　Egg Drop Soup
　　Jahtsai and Meat Soup
　　Velvet Corn and Crab Soup
　　Beef and Lotus Root Soup

One last-minute Stir-Fried or Deep-Fried dish if you are really ambitious

Rice
　　Rice in any form
　　Starchy *Dim Sum* in any form

COCKTAIL PARTIES

Dim Sum and many cured and baked recipes in this book are great for cocktails. Why not try a Western-style cocktail party with Eastern-style food? Choose from the following groupings of dishes.

Food that can be bought from an Oriental Grocer and served cold
　　Shrimp Chips (either already fried, or fried at

home)
　　Smoked Oysters in cottonseed oil, canned
　　Mock Meat, canned
　　Braised Bamboo Shoots, canned
　　Chinese Pickled Onions, in jars
　　Chinese Barbecued Pork (hanging on hooks in Chinese specialty stores; or home-made), cube and serve on toothpicks

Home-made food served cold
　　Tea Eggs
　　Barbecued Spareribs
　　Smoked Spareribs
　　Cantonese Pickles
　　Sichuan Pickled Vegetables
　　Tangy Peppery Cucumbers
　　Smoked Chicken, made from chicken breast, boned and cubed
　　Drunken Chicken, made from chicken breast, boned and cubed
　　Salted Duck, with or without bones
　　Bean Sauce Pork, cubed
　　Lu Beef, cubed
　　Pseudo Smoked Fish

Food that can be kept warm in steamer or on hottray, or re-heated in microwave oven
　　Pearl Balls
　　Silver Thread Rolls

Food that can be kept warm on hottray or in warm oven, or re-heated in microwave oven
　　Sweet and Sour Spareribs
　　Stuffed Mushrooms
　　Scallion Cakes
　　Baked Pork Rolls
　　Guotieh

Food that can be re-heated in a 350°F oven, but preferably refried
　　Spring Rolls (any kind)
　　Shrimp Balls (any kind)
　　Shrimp Toast
　　Fried Wontons
　　Serve the above separately, or combine 7 appetizers on a Seven-Star Platter (See p. 128).

FAMILY-STYLE DINNERS

Unlike at a banquet where the dishes are served one at a time, at a family-style dinner, all the dishes are served simultaneously. Don't let the word "family-style" fool you! You can have banquet-class family-style entertainment right at home!

Sample Menu for Six: The following can be

a party menu or family dinner menu:

Egg Drop Soup
Red-Cooked Beef
Almond Chicken
Tangy Peppery Cucumbers
Boiled Rice
Sesame Cookies

Analysis of the Sample Menu

1. Methods: Six different methods are used in this menu: They are: (1) Plunging, (2) Stewing, (3) Stir-Frying, (4) Pickling, (5) Boiling and (6) Baking.

2. Contrast in Color: Four different colors are used in this menu. They are: (1) Yellow — soup, (2) Reddish-brown — beef, (3) White — chicken, and (4) Green — cucumbers.

3. Contrast in Shape: Four different shapes are used in this menu. They are: (1) Amorphous — soup, (2) Large chunks — beef, (3) Small dices — chicken, and (4) Triangles — cucumbers.

4. Contrast in Texture and Taste: Four different textures and taste are provided by this menu. They are: (1) Soft and bland — Soup, (2) Firm and robust — beef, (3) Delicate and mild — chicken, and (4) Crunchy and pungent — cucumbers.

5. Ease of Early Preparation: Hardly any last-minute hassle. Bake cookies, cook beef and cucumbers ahead of time. Bone, dice chicken and marinate and leave in the refrigerator.

6. Last-Minute Preparation: 30 minutes before dinner, start cooking rice, soak mushrooms. 10 minutes before dinner, reheat beef on slow burner, cook soup and chicken.

Menu Progression:

The following menu list begins with the simple and proceeds to the more elaborate. Use the early menus for family meals and the later ones for entertaining.

Freely interchange recipes in the same Method Group.

Increasing the Servings:

When serving a larger number than indicated, make larger quantities of items designated "L".

Serves 4 or more
Egg Drop Soup
L Barbecued Pork
Stir-Fried Spinach
Boiled Rice

Fruit of the Season

Serves 8 or more
L Fried Spring Chicken
L Lion's Head
Stir-Fried Asparagus
Boiled Rice
Canned Pineapples

Serves 6 or more
L Sweet and Sour Spareribs
Almond Chicken
Cold-Mixed Celery
Boiled Rice
Loquat Mold

Serves 4
Three-Color Soup
Shallow-Fried Fish
Beef and Snowpeas in Oyster Sauce
Cucumber Salad
Boiled Rice
Walnut Cookies

Serves 4 or more
Fish Spring Rolls (appetizer)
L Pork Cutlet in Hoisin Sauce
Silver Chicken Threads
Stir-Fried Bok Choy
Boiled Rice
Almond Doufu

Serves 6 or more
Chicken Slices and Watercress Soup
Sweet and Sour Pork
L Lu Beef
Stir-Fried Cauliflower
Boiled Rice
Eight-Jeweled Rice Pudding

Serves 8
Velvet Corn and Crab Soup
Peking Duck
Pork Shreds in Peking Sauce
Scallion Eggs
Stir-Fried Beansprouts
Thin Cakes
Sesame Cookies and Sherbet

Serves 10 or more
Shrimp Toast (appetizer)
L Fire Pot
Shaobing
Eight-Jewelled Rice Pudding

Serves 8 or more
West Lake Beef Soup
Lemon Chicken

Shrimp with Cashews
L Barbecued Pork
L Asparagus in Oyster Sauce
Boiled Rice
Glutinous Rice Balls

Serves 8 or more
Many Cornered Shrimp Balls (appetizer)
Jahtsai and Meat Slice Soup
L Sweet and Sour Spareribs
Gung Bao Chicken
Shallow-Fried Fish Slices
Cold-Mixed String Beans
Almond Cookies and Ice Cream

Serves 8 or More
Sour Hot Soup
Chicken with Snow Peas
Hunan Steamed Fish
L Pork Cutlet in Hoisin Sauce
Fish-Fragrant Eggplant
Stir-Fried Bok Choy
Steamed Buns
Jujube Fluffy Pastry

BANQUETS

Most banquets are held at restaurants. However, you could do one at home if you can get a few gourmet friends together to help you. Otherwise, you need to set aside 3 or 4 days of hard work.

There are several banquet models. The following model is the one most widely used in Taiwan today. It consists of three parts: appetizers or wine food; main course; and *Dim Sum.*

Appetizers or Wine Food: Can be either an appetizer platter or four separate cold dishes served simultaneously. Choose from Cured, Pickled or Deep-Fried dishes.

Main Course: The main course consists of one elaborate soup dish, followed by 6 to 8 hot dishes. The last of the hot dishes must be a whole fish at the New Year's Day celebrations. All dishes in this group are served in succession.

Dim Sum: Consists of two dishes, one sweet and one savory. They are followed by one sweet soup and a platter of fresh fruit. All dishes in this group are served in succession.

Beverages: Wine, liquor, beer and/or soft drinks are served throughout the meal. Tea is served before the banquet and after, but not during it. Rice is not served at banquets.

SAMPLE MENU

The following is a banquet menu which serves 12. Feel free to interchange dishes in the same METHOD using similar MATERIALS. For instance, the four wine food dishes can be substituted with a single Seven-Star Platter; Lu Beef can be substituted with Bean Sauce Pork; and Spring Rolls can be substituted with Shrimp Toast.

Appetizers: (Served simultaneously in separate small platters)
Pseudo Smoked Fish
Sichuan Bean Sprout Fish Rolls
Lu Beef
Cantonese Pickles

Main Course: (Served in succession)
Shark's Fin Soup
Lemon Chicken
Shrimp and Snow Peas
Cattle Climbing on Trees
Chicken and Watercress Soup
Winter Duet
Hunan Steamed Fish

Dim Sum: (Served in succession)
Eight-Jewelled Rice
Spring Rolls
Almond Doufu
Fruit Platter

CHINESE WINES AND SPIRITS

When the Chinese entertain, *Jiou* is served. *Jiou* is the word for alcoholic beverage, which can be either wine or spirits. Chinese do not have cocktails like the Westerners, and they don't mix their drinks. Ladies usually drink fruity wines while men drink wine, beer or hard liquor.

WHAT KIND OF JIOU TO SERVE

Whether or not to serve wine or spirits, and what kind to serve, is mostly a matter of taste. In China, people usually serve the kind of *Jiou* produced in that area, rather than trying to match the *Jiou* with the food. After all, a Chinese dinner usually includes more than one kind of meat, chicken or fish. In the United States, Shaohsing wine from Taiwan is readily available. Americans enjoy its unusual nutty flavor. Serve it with sour plums or lemon slices. Let each person add the fruit of his choice or drink it plain.

HOW TO SERVE JIOU

Jiou is served when the first appetizer is served, and also all through the meal. *Jiou*, such as Shaohsing, is never served chilled, but is heated by placing the bottle or wine pot in a pot of very hot water. Serve it in porcelain cups instead of wine glasses. Use small cups for the spirits and large cups for the wine.

ALL THE TEA IN CHINA

It is said that one *liang* (a little more than one ounce) of the best tea is worth one *liang* of gold. Chinese savor tea the way French savor wine.

One drinks tea before dinner, after dinner, between dinners, but not at dinner. This is the practice in most provinces. In restaurants in Taiwan and Mainland China, tea is served the moment you sit down at the table. The tea cups disappear when the main dishes are brought in. They appear again when you finish the dinner. One exception is that with *Dim Sum* tea is always served, but tea snacks are not dinners.

What liquid is used at a Chinese meal? Wines and liquors are served at banquets as are beer and soda. There are always many soups: sweet and savory soups, clear and thick soups, plain and fancy soups... Sweet soups are served between two main dishes to refresh your palate, and to prepare you for further adventures in exotic dining. For family meals, at least one soup is served, except when you have a one-dish meal, such as Fire Pot, which is a meal by itself. The soup is the only liquid at family meals. Tea or water are usually not served.

However, a pot of tea sits on the table in every Chinese restaurant overseas. This is because the Cantonese, the ones who first introduced Chinese food to the West, drank tea at the table and brought the custom with them.

A cup of tea is always the sign of a "warm" welcome, not only in homes and restaurants, but also in offices and on trains, sometimes even in shops. In a tea house, you can buy a cup of tea and the waiter will always fill your cup whenever it gets low. You can sit there for hours to discuss business or to keep up with the latest gossip.

VARIETIES OF TEA

There are endless varieties of tea. Since tea is not used during the meal, there is no protocol for tea in China as there is for wine in the West. Therefore, use the tea you enjoy the most.

RED TEA

Red Tea, which the Westerners call black tea, is either semi-fermented or fermented. Actually it is neither red nor black, but different shades of reddish brown, depending on the degree of fermentation. Some are called just red tea, others are specified as Jasmine, Oolong (Dark Dragon), Teh Kuan Yin (Iron Goddess of Mercy) or Lichee (scented with lichee flavor), etc.

Oolong and Jasmine are the favorite Chinese teas of Americans. They are semi-fermented. Jasmine is scented with Jasmine blossoms. But in the best Jasmine tea one should not see any blossoms.

GREEN TEA

Green Tea is unfermented. You have to cultivate a taste for it. It is a tea drinker's tea. Generations of scholars and poets have savored it. Long after you sip it, the glow of contentment lingers on. The best green tea is the first crop picked in the early spring. *Loong Jing* (Dragon Well) is the best known green tea. Like the green vegetables which should be eaten green, green tea is brewed uncovered, and should be consumed before it turns brown.

CHRYSANTHEMUM TEA

Unlike the other flower teas which come with the flowers or flower scent, Chrysanthemum Tea is made by adding to tea the little daisy-like flowers which can be purchased from a Chinese grocer. The tea used is usually green. Add a few flowers to each teaspoon of tea leaves to make one cup of tea. The flowers will open in boiling water. This tea not only tastes good, but also looks pretty and smells fragrant. Occasionally the Cantonese put rock candy in this tea. For those who cannot take caffeine, use one teaspoon of chrysanthemums alone in a cup of boiling water to make a delightful hot beverage. It is also believed to make one sleep better at night.

HOW TO MAKE SUPER TEA

BUY TOP QUALITY TEA LEAVES

KEEP TEA LEAVES IN AN AIRTIGHT CAN

Keep your tea leaves in an airtight can. The best tea can comes with both an inner and an outer lid. Buy the smallest quantity unless you are a regular tea drinker.

USE HEAVY UTENSILS

Although it is not necessary to preheat a teapot, tea brews better in a pot or a mug rather than in a thin cup. Water cools too fast in a thin cup for the tea to brew properly.

USE PROPER AMOUNT

Use proportionally less tea leaves per cup for larger quantity of tea. The following is only a guide. You have to experiment to determine the amount that suits your taste best:

For an 8-cup teapot, use 2 level tablespoons of tea leaves.

For a 12-ounce mug, use 1 level teaspoon of tea leaves.

MAKE SURE THE WATER IS BOILING

This means that you can hear a whistling tea kettle scream like a siren, or you can see **large** bubbles surfacing. A noisy kettle quiets down slightly when it boils.

METHOD

Place tea leaves in a mug or a teapot, fill 1/4 full with boiling water. Immediately drain and discard liquid. Fill the container with boiling water. Serve after 5 minutes.

Refill with boiling water when the container is 1/4 full. Keep on refilling until the tea is too weak, about 2 to 3 times.

AT THE TABLE

CHOPSTICK MANNERS OR, DO EVERYTHING YOUR MOTHER TOLD YOU NOT TO DO!

Don't be afraid of chopsticks!

If you can use a pencil, you can use chopsticks. One of my students in the Beginner's Course came to class one night, and declared that she cooked a Chinese dinner for her 78-year-old mother-in-law. The mother-in-law wouldn't let fork and knife spoil a perfectly good Chinese meal, and insisted on learning how to use the chopsticks — and she did!

Here's how to use chopsticks:

Keep the lower chopstick stationary and the upper moveable as follows:
① Hold the upper chopstick as you would a pencil or pen. ② Slide the lower chopstick through the arch of your hand and rest on the fourth finger. ③ Pick up food by moving the tip of the upper toward the lower.

Things your mother told you not to do — but you should do...

* Your mother told you to twist spaghetti around your fork and eat it, never slurp. But at the Chinese table, you pick up the noodles with chopsticks and daintily slurp them down.

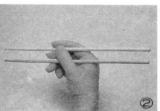

*Your mother told you not to bite anything off of a fork. But at the Chinese table it is proper to bite food off of chopsticks.

*Your mother told you to sit straight at the table and bring the fork to your mouth. At the Chinese table, you lift the rice bowl and gently incline your head as you respect its providers.

*Your mother told you to say "pass the potatoes please!" But at the Chinese table it is impolite to ask someone to pass a dish to you. You may reach, particularly so that you may serve someone else. If you are too shy or too polite, you can eat just what is within reach, and what others put on your plate.

*Your mother told you to mind your manners and help yourself to reasonable portions. Of course, never reach. But at the Chinese table, you observe a different set of rules. You reach with your chopsticks. You heap the best morsels — not on your plate, but on the plates of the ones to whom you want to show honor or affection. Growing up in wartime China, we sisters would let each other have a chance to select the food, suppressing the urge to grab for ourselves. Under war-time scarcities, the race to give up the best pieces really demonstrated sacrificial giving. With today's abundance of food, there is less sacrifice associated with putting food on other people's plates, but you still feel a warm glow when you offer food to others at the table, and vice versa.

The Chinese child is taught to be thoughtful of others from an early age. He is taught to let others enjoy the choicest dish and the choicest morsels.

*Your hostess assigns your seat at the table. At the Chinese table, you fight — against, not for it! The idea is to honor someone else above you; and you give up your honored seat to someone else — saying in effect: "You are more worthy than I am to occupy that seat!"

*Your mother told you never to ask anybody's age. But in China it is good manners to ask some real old person's age. You ask: "How tall is your longevity?" And watch a big smile spread across the respondent's wrinkles when he (she) computes the actual age, adds a year before birth, and another for the first New Year, and a liberal dash of longevity license, and announces his (her) age. You applaud the veteran of years by bowing and saying: "The heavens have indeed blessed you!"

*Your mother taught you to compliment people on their beautiful clothes. But in China, the one complimented may feel like offering you the object of your admiration. You could end up collecting a wardrobe (not necessarily in your size or style!).

TABLE-SETTING, SEATING AND ETIQUETTE

Ancestor's Spirit Plate: Ancestors are worshipped by the Chinese. A carved wooden plate on which the names of the departed grandparents or parents are inscribed is given the highest place of honor in the house. The direction of the house is determined geomantically, and so is the direction of the front door. As you enter the front door, you face the ancestral plate.

Order is the quintessence of Chinese society. And the "seat"(ing) is in descending order: Heaven, Earth, King, Parents and Teachers. Since the founding of the Republic of China in 1911, "King" is replaced by "Country." Finding the "Country" too abstract a concept, it has recently been substituted by "Friends," of course at a lower order. You may have the plate of one or both of your parents, or grandparents, or a plate which says: "Heaven, Earth, Parents, Teachers and Friends." At the table, directly below the plate is the place of honor which is occupied by the parents unless grandparents are present. At contemporary ceremonial banquets, temporary plates are made up in the absence of permanent plates.

The Host and the Guest of Honor: At the banquet, the guest of honor is seated at seat #1 directly opposite the host, who occupies the last seat, #12. The guest of honor sits facing the door, which is the position occupied by the head of the household at the family table. The second most-honored guest sits to the right of the guest of honor, at seat #2, and the third most-honored guest sits to the left of the guest of honor, at seat #3, etc. (see next page).

Seating Etiquette: Except in the rare instance of pre-assigned seats at a large banquet, you are expected to engage in friendly fights to honor each other by offering the better seat. It is perfectly polite to address someone your junior as "elder brother," and offer him a higher seat – which is closer to the seat of honor – but it would be bad form for him to accept an undeserved honor.

Door

Old is Beautiful: Would you believe that you honor someone by calling him "older brother?" Age before beauty is certainly taken seriously in China. Presumably, in ancient days of short life expectancy, every year lived was an added mark of heaven's blessings, making the really old highly venerated. Wisdom is associated with age. Therefore, your addressing someone as senior to you — notice the older "brother" or "sister" form of address — and deferring to him or her in the honor of a higher seat at the table is a sign of respect. Think of different reasons why you should respect someone: "How do I honor thee — Let me count the ways!" After a respectable vying to honor each other, you take a seat with proper reluctance, saying " 恭敬 不如 從命": "Obedience is better than deference."

Table-setting: As Omar Khayyam would have said: "A simple bowl, a pair of chopsticks and thou beside me." The rice bowl is on the left; the pair of chopsticks to the right. You put food from the serving plates into your rice bowl. In addition, you can place a small plate in front of the bowl with a China spoon next to it, so the food can be placed on the plate. The hot towels of the old days have been replaced by modern napkins.

No Center-piece: Every dish is a work of art; therefore, the Chinese table has no centerpiece. You need bright lights to appreciate the succession of delectable delights; therefore, no Chinese dinners by candle light.

Eating and Drinking: Conspicuous by its absence at the family table is the glass. Soup is the liquid at the Chinese table, not beverages or water. Soup is the only liquid at the family table. At the banquet table glasses are provided for beer, wine and soft drinks.

Serving Order: The host toasts the guests as each new dish is brought to the table. The guest of honor reaches with his chopsticks first, so that the other guests can follow suit.

Toasting: No water is served, but wine is. At a banquet, you toast the host, and each guest in turn, until you have toasted everybody at least once. You never drink alone at the table. Usually the host offers the first and the last toast to all the guests. You do not take a sip without toasting or being toasted.

Nothing to Eat! is the traditional opening statement of the host as you sit down at the table, groaning with delicacies. That is the politeness of the humble host who is saying how honored he is to have you honor his house by partaking in something which cannot compare with the high honor of your presence.

Oohs and Aahs: Chinese banquet dishes are served in succession. You partake of each dish, and then the next one appears. Take time to look at the new dish, and your oohs and aahs will be spontaneous! Comment on the beauty, the fragrance, the texture, and the taste.

No Good: The host will promptly discount your praise and protest that the food is no good. He will not thank you for your compliments because accepting compliments is considered immodest. My father tells a story which shows what happens when the shoe is on the other foot. At the end of an excellent banquet, the host praised the excellent food, but one guest insisted that the food was no good, to the utter astonishment of everyone present. It turned out that the host had borrowed the chef from that particular guest – who was being polite in not accepting the praise for his excellent chef!

Conclusion: The guest of honor is the first to leave the banquet. If it is a "no-host" banquet, you will find the guests vigorously fighting with each other at the cashier's counter. Don't worry, they are not complaining about the bill; instead, they are fighting for the honor to pay for the dinner for everyone. Chinese never go Dutch; after all, they are Chinese, not Dutch!

INDEX

RECIPES BY FOOD GROUPINGS